Patrick, Sir Geddes

Chapters in modern Botany

Patrick, Sir Geddes

Chapters in modern Botany

ISBN/EAN: 9783743331303

Manufactured in Europe, USA, Canada, Australia, Japa

Cover: Foto ©ninafisch / pixelio.de

Manufactured and distributed by brebook publishing software (www.brebook.com)

Patrick, Sir Geddes

Chapters in modern Botany

CONTENTS

CHAPTER I

PITCHER PLANTS

Darlingtonia — Sarracenia — Origin of Darlingtonia Pitchers — Insect-Catching — Other Relations to Insects — Minute Structure of these Pitchers — Australian Pitcher Plant (Cephalotus) — The Pitcher Plant proper (Nepenthes) — Secreting Glands and Nectaries . . . . . . Pages 1-20

CHAPTER II

PITCHER PLANTS — *continued*

Use of Pitchers, "Bionomics" — Bionomics — Bionomics of Nepenthes — Morphology of the Pitcher — Bladderwort — Bionomics of Bladderwort — Allied Forms 21-35

CHAPTER III

OTHER INSECTIVOROUS PLANTS — DIFFICULTIES AND CRITICISMS

Fly-Traps (Dionæa and Aldrovanda) — Sundews and Birdlime Traps — Butterworts — Sundews proper (Drosera) — Details, Functional and Structural — Digestion — Movements — Ab-

sorption — Utility — Other Insectivorous Plants — Legends — Difficulties — Further Difficulties and Criticisms — Direction of further Investigation; Possible Compromise . Pages 36–59

CHAPTER IV

MOVEMENT AND NERVOUS ACTION IN PLANTS

Climbing Plants — Darwin's Observations, with Summary — Interpretation of Movements — Movements of Seedlings — Methods of Observation — Theory of Circumnutation . . 60–75

CHAPTER V

MOVEMENTS OF PLANTS — *continued*

Movements in relation to Gravitation — Light-seeking and Light-avoiding Movements — Rationale of Light-seeking and Light-avoiding Movements — The Sleep of Plants — Mr. Francis Darwin's recent Discussion of Plant Movements — Summary and Conclusion 76–94

CHAPTER VI

THE WEB OF LIFE

Struggle among Plants — Perched Plants or Epiphytes — Parasitic Plants — Mistleto — Dodder — Root-Parasites — Toothwort — Broom-rapes — Saprophytes — Parasitic Fungi — Bacteria — Symbiosis 95–119

CHAPTER VII

RELATIONS BETWEEN PLANTS AND ANIMALS

Plants and Snails — Plants and Ants — Domatia — Myrmecodia — Galls — Plants and Aphides — Cats and Clover . 120–142

CHAPTER VIII

SPRING AND ITS STUDIES — GEOGRAPHICAL DISTRIBUTION AND WORLD-LANDSCAPES — SEEDLING AND BUD

Spring Studies — Mode of Study in Botany — Phenology and Distribution — Aspects of Nature, Vegetation and Landscapes of the World — Germination — Buds and Bud-Scales — Arrangement of Leaves in the Bud . . Pages 143–160

CHAPTER IX

LEAVES

General Facts in regard to the Life of Leaves — Experiments, rough and exact — Summary of Leaf Functions — The Structure of the Leaf — Palisade Cells and Chlorophyll Grains — Shapes of Leaves — Leaves adapted to special Functions — Substitutes for Leaves — Vitality of the Leaf — Fall of the Leaf . 161–189

CHAPTER X

SUGGESTIONS FOR FURTHER STUDY

Root and Stem — Flower, Fruit, and Seed — The Web of Life once more — Systematic Botany — Morphology of Organs and Tissues — Evolution 190–201

LIST OF ILLUSTRATIONS

A Tropical Forest . . . . *Frontispiece*

FIG.   PAGE
1. *Darlingtonia californica* 3
2. Leaves of *Sarracenia purpurea* 9
3. Pitcher of *Nepenthes distillatoria* 16
4. Pitcher of *Nepenthes bicalcarata* showing downward-directed prickles 27
5. Elk's-horn Fern (*Platycerium grande*) 99
6. Patch of Lichen grown synthetically by Bonnier (from sowing of fungus spores on algæ) under bacteriological precautions against entrance of foreign spores . 117
7. Assai Palm (*Euterpe oleracia*) 156
8. Apparatus of Bonnier and Mangin, for analysis of gases given off by plants 166

CHAPTER I

PITCHER PLANTS

Darlingtonia — Sarracenia — Origin of Darlingtonia Pitchers — Insect-Catching — Other Relations to Insects — Minute Structure of these Pitchers — Australian Pitcher Plant (Cephalotus) — The Pitcher Plant proper (Nepenthes) — Secreting Glands as Nectaries.

IN attempting to arrange a suitable introduction to the study of botany, a teacher may incline to one or other of two distinct methods. The first, and in many ways the more satisfactory, is to take the commonest plants around one, begin with the simplest knowledge of these, extend it by what is easily to be observed or obtained, deepen this by closer study, and next extend to less familiar forms the growing experience and practical power of the student. Most courses of biological instruction now actually run upon this principle: they place before the student some common type, some frog or crayfish, some common fern and flower, from which he may work his way towards a wider survey of the science. The other method, which also has its favourable side, is to start with something rare or strange — at any rate unfamiliar, — and so not only evade the prejudice that botany deals mainly in hard names or the like, but obtain the immense advantage of ministering to some measure of reawakened curiosity, some freshened feeling of the varied marvellousness of nature.

The plan here adopted is practically a compromise of the two. Beginning indeed with some of the strangest forms and processes of the vegetable world, it is not proposed to exhibit these merely as a vegetable menagerie of rarities and wonders, but to use them as a convenient means of reaching, as speedily as may be, not only (*a*) some general comprehension of the processes and knowledge of the forms of vegetable life, but also, and from the very first, (*b*) some intelligent grasp of the experimental methods and reasoning employed in their investigation. For these purposes a very convenient beginning may be made with pitcher plants.

Moreover, they will be found to lead us more rapidly than would many more familiar types to the point of view of Darwin, and the reading of his actual works; this being of course most central and characteristic in modern botany.

Darlingtonia. — Beginning then far afield, in the land of big trees and vegetable wonders, we find not the least of these in a marsh plant discovered just fifty years ago by the botanist of an exploring expedition in the region of the Sierra Nevada. A fresh expedition nine years later gathered flowering specimens, but it was not until 1855 that the systematist Torrey formally introduced the plant to the world as *Darlingtonia californica* (the surname given in compliment to a friend). At first a rarity of botanic gardens, it is now not uncommon in greenhouses, and is very easy of cultivation. The flowers are large and strange, resembling those of *Sarracenia*, described below (p. 5). The leaves, however, are yet stranger; they rise in stemless clumps above their mossy bed to a height of 12 or 18 inches, slender tubes extending upwards like organ pipes, but each recurving into a large and well-arched hood or helmet, with a framework of strongly-marked veins. This helmet is brightly splashed with red, and glistens with innumerable translucent spaces in which green

FIG. 1.— *Darlingtonia californica.*

tissue is absent, and only the epidermis of either side remains. Its small downward-directed opening is concealed, not only by its position, but by a gaily-tinted and banner-like streamer which hangs in front. To this opening, however, there ascends a gently-curved pathway which runs upwards from the very ground, as if expressly built for ants and other wingless creepers, while at its top it is no less useful as a landing stage for winged explorers. The finger-tip can easily be inserted, and finds the edge to be incurved all the way round, while the descent into the pitcher is of course close by. Slitting open one of the old pitchers a gruesome sight presents itself—two, five, nay, it may be more likely twenty or fifty mouldering corpses, chiefly, in our greenhouses at least, those of bluebottles and wasps, but with now and then also a moth or bee.

Sarracenia. — To understand all these peculiarities of form and life we may best pass to the allied genus *Sarracenia*, of which there are a good many different species of similar habit and habitat, but wider distribution, the genus ranging from Florida to Canada. The form is less perplexing, the hollow leaves are now simply trumpet-shaped, and instead of being rolled through a semicircle and curiously narrowed, open widely towards the sky, while the forked pennon of Darlingtonia is obviously represented by an almost circular or somewhat pointed leafy expansion, sometimes sloping over the mouth, like a half open lid or cover, large enough to throw off rain, but often also standing erect and conspicuous, the whole effect being often no less attractive to botanist or bluebottle than that of the Darlingtonia itself (Fig. 1, p. 3). Here clearly we have the simple form; and passing from the empirical facts of geographical distribution towards that interpretation the healthy childish or scientific mind cannot but demand, we can hardly fail to suspect that Darlingtonia is but the most outlying of the Sarracenias, one which has wandered to the farther side of the Rocky Mountains, and in that region become so much specialised beyond the ordinary type as to warrant re-naming as a new genus. Comparing the flowers, we find essential kinship yet sufficient generic difference; curiously enough, it is the flower of Sarracenia which is the more specialised. Each is solitary upon its lofty stalk, the long dull-red petals quite surpassed in conspicuousness by the curiously-dilated style, recalling the peltate leaf of the common Indian Cress (*Tropæolum*), which climbs over so many cottage walls, or in dwarf forms brightens the garden border. In Darlingtonia the style merely shows the faintest beginnings of such an arrangement. From this one of the perplexities of evolution becomes evident; we often cannot say that one plant is more evolved than another as a whole; but only it may be on this or that respect, *e.g.* the form of the leaf in Darlingtonia, of style in Sarracenia.

Origin of Darlingtonia Pitchers. — But how should such a change come about? the thoughtful student will ask, so beginning to raise all the enigmas of evolution. Was it by change of climate and soil? or by spontaneous internal variations, trifling differences of the kind visible in every patch of seedlings, of which some, useful in some way to the plant, helped their lucky possessors, which therefore survived while their fellows died, and transmitted these to a new series of similar divergent seedlings, which again had to struggle for life in the same way? Thus we see how in course of generations we might obtain important and obvious differences from the simpler parent form; and this of course would have been Darwin's view; it is a special case of his famous theory of "the Origin of Species, by means of Natural Selection, or the Preservation of Fortunate Variations in the Struggle for Life," while the speculation as to the possible but unknown influence of climate and soil represents the position of the earlier evolutionists, Lamarck, Erasmus Darwin, etc. Here, then, at the very outset of our studies, the riddle of origins comes up and refuses to admit itself fully solved. For though each of these answers alone successively satisfied many minds, Darwin himself at least inclined towards some varying compromise of them. And as the student learns the really scientific attitude, that of not learning answers but of asking questions, new puzzles arise. Thus, what influence are we to place upon the geographical isolation through many generations of the incipient Darlingtonia from its kindred Sarracenias? How far does it modify our natural selectionist position with its characteristic insistance upon adaptation to external uses when we note that the odd hood of the Darlingtonia is developed merely by increasing the relative rate of growth of the outer and upper surface of the Sarracenia pitcher, especially as we approach its mid-rib, so producing not only the inflation but the curvature, and even the stretching apart of the leaf-tissue so as to leave the pretty window-like patches? But if this be clear we have already got a step below the conventional Darwinian level of external adaptation, below the idea of progress merely through the cumulative patenting of mechanical improvements in our fly-traps. Helpful though that explanation is, so far as it goes, we have in fact reached a new and deeper plane of thought on which it may become necessary to work out an entirely new set of evolutionary interpretations. The outer world of external and mechanical adaptations once left behind, we are at once brought face to face with the internal and vital processes, and have to grapple with the problems of organic growth, both general and special; in other words, it is in terms of the laws of growth that we have to reinterpret the phenomena of development. We are familiar with these differences of growth of different regions of the leaf, as in young leaves of ferns, but the experimental study in detail lies still before us. Deliberately to arrange new conditions for our Sarracenia so that it shall at least begin to roll its leaf into the form of Darlingtonia is, however, at present "impracticable," *i.e.* remains a problem for the experimental physiologist. Yet even the natural selectionist most satisfied with accounting for the change on the principle of the mechanically improving fly-trap is notwithstanding the very man empirically to help, if not anticipate us, by finding us a seedling varying in the required direction among a patch of young Sarracenia; for on this and its offspring the experimentalist might best begin. All such experimental researches are as yet only in their infancy, but it is becoming admitted on all hands that as the past of the science lies mainly in systematic collections, in anatomical and microscopic analyses, so its future has to be sought in the physiological laboratory, the greenhouse, and the garden.

Insect-Catching.—But how, the active minded observer will ask, does our curious helmet-like Darlingtonia pitcher keep its victims,—for though it is natural for an insect to creep into what doubtless appears to it a very inviting new kind of flower, why should it not creep out again? A first difficulty is afforded by the incurved margins; but this would not be enough to detain it; and here comes in the use of the relatively widely distended helmet-space with its innumerable transparent glassy panes let into its whole upper surface. The insect has eyes on the top and sides of its head, and sees abundant light above to spread its wings and beat itself upon the resisting roof and walls of the pitcher as persistently and as vainly as he does within our own window-casement. No doubt when he becomes tired and falls down over the entrance he may at times escape, but is more likely only to rest over it till he can again begin his struggles on the wing, while the adjacent opening, that of the fatal oubliette, is not only of much larger diameter, but of gently-sloping sides instead of repellent recurved margins. The walls of the leaf-tube substantially correspond to those of Sarracenia, which we may therefore describe more minutely.

The gaily-coloured lid of the Sarracenia pitcher is bedewed in spring and early summer with drops of nectar, which lie on its inward surface, at least for the most part; not on both, as in the pennon of the Darlingtonia. A closer examination of its surface shows that these drops are at once helped to form, and if sufficiently large to trickle downwards by a coating of fine but short and stiff hairs which arise from the epidermic surface. Here, in fact, is in every way an admirably-constructed "attractive surface," and it is obvious as well as natural that the insects which sip the honey should travel down into the interior of the pitcher to seek for more. Beyond the lid surface with its hairs and nectar-glands they come upon the smooth and glassy "conducting surface," a well-paved path leading indeed towards destruction. In *S. purpurea* there are indeed a few fresh nectaries to be reached by this descent, a new secreting surface below the conducting one—in *S. flava* and other species not even this,—but in all cases we soon reach the "detentive surface" of the whole lower part of the pitcher. This is covered with long, stout, bristly hairs, averaging say ¼ inch long, all sloping downwards into the cavity of the pitcher, and so presenting no obstacle towards descent, but much resistance towards return, as the finger can easily verify, or as the dead inmates of the tubular prison still more conclusively show. That so comparatively powerful an insect as a wasp or bluebottle can be thus detained may be at first sight perplexing; but we see that there is no scope to use the wings for escape, while legs and wings alike become entangled and held back by the stiffly-pointed hairs, which the struggling insect can at most only thrust along, and thus not break. Another captive soon comes on top;

ventilation becomes checked, and the foul air rising from dead predecessors must still further check respiration; little wonder then that life must fail. Even in our greenhouses

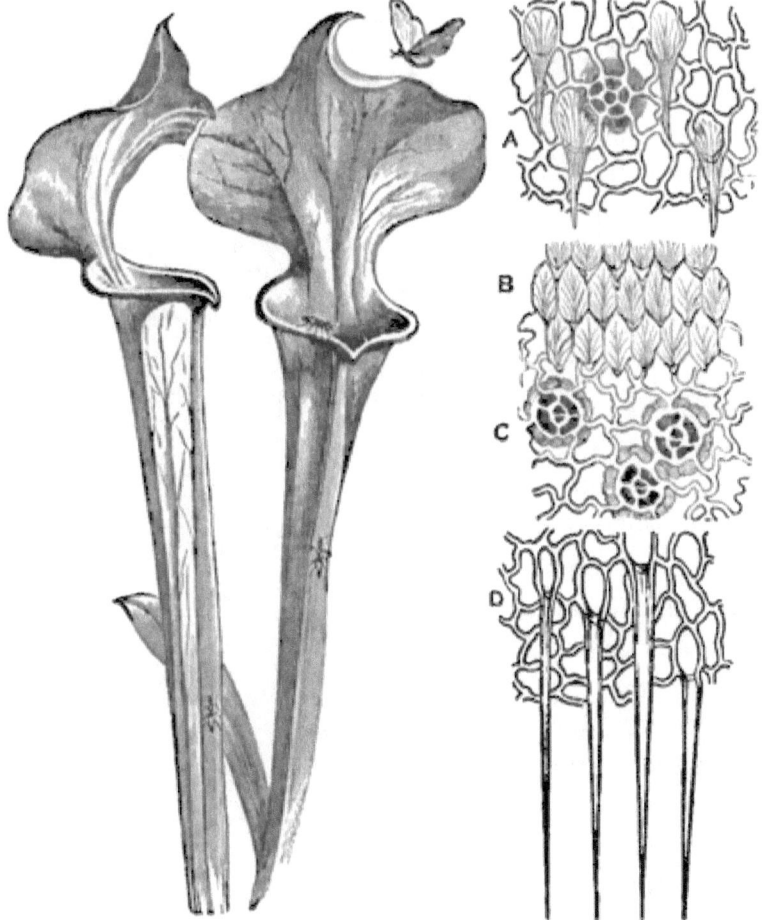

FIG. 2. — Leaves of *Sarracenia purpurea*. A, attractive surface of lid; B, conducting; C, glandular, and D, detentive surface, magnified. (A and D are taken from *S. flava*.)

the leaf thus becomes filled, not only 1 or 2, but often 5 or 6 inches deep with dead insects; while observers on the spot, notably Dr. Mellichamp, to whom our knowledge is mainly due, have shown that there is normally a considerable amount of fluid secreted by the pitcher, although this does not seem to appear in European cultivation, and that this fluid has distinctly anæsthetic and fatal properties to insects immersed in it.

Other Relations to Insects.—It is an odd fact that while with us the bluebottle falls an easy and natural prey to this unwonted trap, being doubtless attracted like the wasp by that odour of decomposing carrion to which the bee and butterfly in turn owe their safety, a shrewder American cousin (*Sarcophaga sarraceniæ*) lays a few eggs over the pitcher edge, where the maggots hatch and fatten on the abundant food. In April three or four of these larvæ are to be found, but in June or July only one survives, the victor who has devoured his brethren. But nemesis is often at hand in the form of a grub-seeking bird, who slits up the pitcher with his beak, and makes short work of all its eatable contents. For this bird in turn the naturalist has next to lie in wait, and so add a new link to the chain.

The larvæ of a moth (*Xanthoptera semicrocea*) also inhabit the pitcher, but devour its tissue, not its animal inmates; in fact, they spin a web across its diameter, as if to exclude further entrance of these, and then devour the upper part of the tissue; especially, it would seem, the nectar-glands, finally passing through their chrysalis stage within the cavity of the pitcher, and not, as in the case of the *Sarcophaga* larva, making their exit into the ground.

It is said that spiders also spin their webs over the mouths of the pitchers and wait to reap the profit of their attractiveness—again a point of almost human shrewdness.

An American entomologist, Professor Riley, has described the ways in which these associated living insects (*commensals*, we may perhaps call them, by a not extreme stretch of technical language) are adapted to life in such dangerous conditions. The moth has long spurs upon its tibiæ (second leg joints), which cross many of the hairs as it walks, and so prevent its legs from sinking among them; while its larvæ, destitute of this snow-shoe arrangement, spin their silken strands over the tips of the detentive hairs, and so keep out of danger. The larvæ of the blow-fly, on the other hand, have peculiarly long claws and large cushions on the last tarsal joints, and so grip down through the hairs and hook themselves firmly into the very tissue of the trumpet-leaf itself.

The question naturally arose—are not these treacherous plants victimising the very insects which fertilise them? But this seems little or not at all to be the case; for *S. variolaris*, at least, our good observer Dr. Mellichamp has shown that fertilisation is effected by the "melancholy chafer" (*Euphoria melancholica*), nor has he ever beheld the moth *Xanthoptera* so act. So far, at any rate, it seems we have quite distinct and separate inter-adaptations of flower and leaf, and two distinct and separate insects.

Minute Structure of the Pitcher.—Before leaving this subject one may have a useful first lesson in "vegetable histology," since the tissues here are not only peculiarly interesting and intelligible, but very easily handled. Opening the pitcher with one's penknife it is easy to make out with the naked eye, and clear with the pocket lens, the essential character of these surfaces, attractive, conductive, and detentive respectively; but to see the exquisite beauty and perfection of their details we must multiply lens above lens, so developing our simple microscope, noting, of course, that we are passing to no separate "science of microscopy," but that we are merely adding in front of our own eye lens first one artificial lens, and then more as we need them. How these lenses need to be held together, and how one combination of these is brought near the eye ("eye-piece"), so as to multiply still further the image already magnified by another held nearer the object (and hence naturally termed object-glass), is of course the elementary common sense of that exquisite marvel of detailed perfection, the compound microscope. The further developments, as that of shutting off side light above the object-glass by the microscope tube, and below it by the stage-diaphragm, of placing the object upon a transparent stage, and this upon a perforated one, or of getting the instrument when we wish to examine a transparent object out of the inconvenient horizontal position at first necessary into the more convenient vertical or sloping one by the simple device of reflecting the window light through the tube to the eye by means of a mirror fixed below the stage, are again no less obvious. This elementary instrument once constructed, a new set of considerations would naturally arise, among which the necessity of focussing and the difficulty of getting rid of the prismatic colours which would as yet enhalo our magnified image may be cited as specially important. These have to be met by mechanical and optical devices respectively, which are familiar enough; and so we might work on, a whole volume being needed to do justice to the history of the instrument, as, indeed, are special journals to its unending developments. The bare outline given above is but to emphasise the idea, commonplace in phrase but too little habitual in practice, that the scientific study of anything, be it a natural or social product, ought always to proceed from the known towards the unknown, and rationally from its beginnings onwards wherever possible.

Given, then, the compound microscope, we may first attempt to examine the epidermis more in detail, beginning with the attractive surface of the lid by shaving off thin slices from its surface, and mounting them in a drop of water between slide and cover-glass. These, however, we probably find to be comparatively opaque and confused, because too thick, and including much of the deeper leaf-tissue or parenchyma as well as epidermis. We may, it is true, improve our preparation by the use of methods familiar to every microscopist, *e.g.* by washing the preparation in spirit to dissolve out the green colouring matter or chlorophyll, by treatment with caustic potash solution to destroy even the protoplasm, by dyeing or staining the cell-walls conveniently with a solution of one of the anilines to bring out their outlines more clearly, and by mounting in glycerine instead of water, so as to give greater transparency to the whole. Instead of all this trouble, which after all will not make a good preparation out of a badly-made section, we may learn much from even a thick slice in the fresh state by observing merely its edges, which are sure to be somewhere thin enough. A better method however, which, with a little practice, will be found to give excellent preparations, not only of all the tougher-leaved insectivorous plants, but of any tolerably strong epidermis, is to lay the morsel of leaf face downwards upon a slide in a large drop of water, and then holding it firmly at one edge, to scrape away with a sharp scalpel or penknife the other epidermis and the green leaf-tissue, the veins too, as far as they will come, washing the debris from the preparation from time to time, and scraping more carefully and lightly as the lower epidermis is exposed, and of course threatens or begins to tear. When tolerably clean the preparation may be turned over and examined, a fundamental principle in all microscopic study being first to make out all one can with the low magnifying power before proceeding to a higher one, while the various operations of histological "*cuisine*" above indicated may be applied if desired, and the preparation mounted permanently for the collection, either simply in glycerine by putting a ring of asphalt or gold size around the cover-glass edge, or by mounting in glycerine jelly. Sufficient technical skill and experience to make very fair botanical preparations will be found to come very rapidly with practice, especially if the beginner can obtain a practical start from any more experienced student or amateur; the help of any work on the microscope is often of much value, although there is nowadays a bewildering wealth of technical devices, each no doubt useful in its own way, like the numberless refinements of the microscope itself, yet like these quite unnecessary until skill has been reached and special problems undertaken.

Australian Pitcher Plant (Cephalotus). — Another pitcher plant, farther-fetched than Darlingtonia, and less frequent in cultivation in our greenhouse collections — indeed one of the rarest and most peculiar plants in the world — is the curious little Australian pitcher plant *Cephalotus follicularis*, which occurs only in a small area not far from the capital of Western Australia. It is by far the smallest and least impressive of all the pitcher plants, yet is of some beauty, and also of morphological interest in possessing at once ordinary leaves and well-formed pitchers between which no gradations normally exist. In the large collection of pitchered and other insectivorous plants in the Edinburgh Botanic Garden the late Professor Dickson (than whom these interesting forms have never had a more keen and thoughtful student) was able to collect and figure an interesting series of the monstrous leaves which occasionally arise, and thus to show that the pitcher is but a specialised modification of the ordinary leaf, a first embryonic dimple near the point deepening backwards and downwards into a pouch, the lid thus arising on the side of the pitcher orifice originally nearer the base of the leaf. The histological details of the pitcher are of interest, and of exceptional beauty of colour.

The Pitcher Plant proper (Nepenthes).— From this solitary and tiny Australian rarity we may now pass to the abundant and magnificent pitcher plants proper, the genus *Nepenthes*, of which not less than forty species are described in Dr. Macfarlane's recent excellent revision of the group. They are widely scattered over the Oriental tropics, with their headquarters in the hotter regions of the Malay Archipelago, but thence range northward into Cochin China, southwards into North Australia, and westwards into Ceylon, Bengal, and even Madagascar. In all the species the pitcher is borne at the end of a long tendril-like prolongation of the leaf, and is not only of very beautiful form but great size, varying from an inch to a foot or more in depth. Two varieties of pitcher occur in many species, the first, associated with the lower leaves and developed during the younger state of the plants, are not uncommonly found actually resting on the ground. This form is short and broad, provided with broad, external, wing-like prolongations, up which ants and other ground insects readily make their way to the lip of the pitcher. The adult and more abundant form of pitcher is longer and narrower, with the external wing-like appendages less strongly developed, or it may be even absent. The anterior (lower) surface of the lid stands well open, serving after maturity no longer as a protective cover, save that it may serve to throw off rain, but apparently as an attractive surface or insect lure, being, like that of the forms already examined, more or less baited with nectar. The rim of the pitcher rewards the closest scrutiny, its surface being beautifully fluted and turned inwards and downwards, so as not only to strengthen the pitcher and keep its mouth always stiffly open, but to lead the insect gently to the dangerous verge, at which the fluid contents of the pitcher come fully into view, and the glassy conducting surface can be easily reached. Dickson discovered also the apparently constant presence of a row

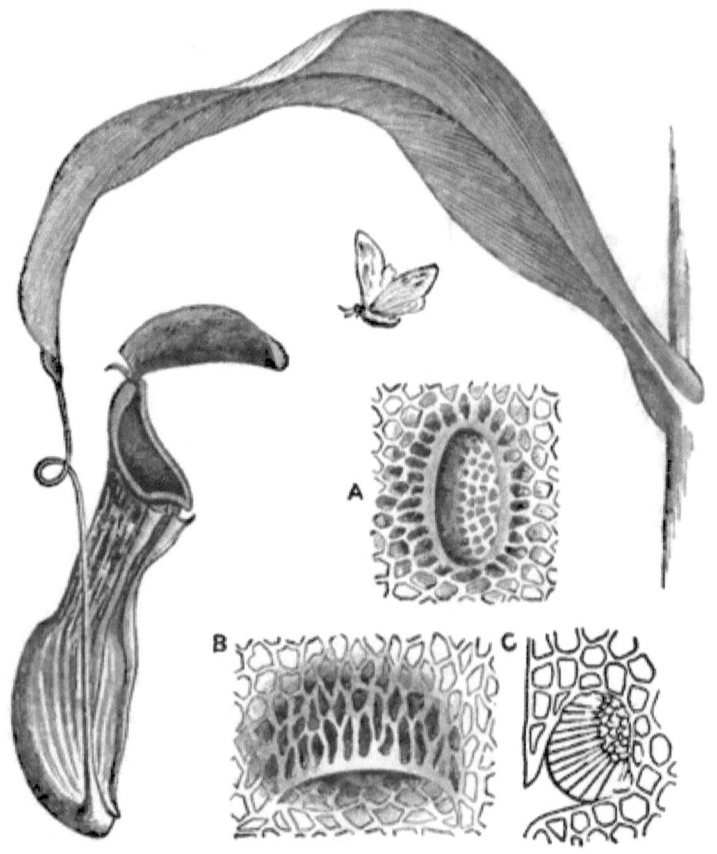

FIG. 3.—Pitcher of *Nepenthes distillatoria*. A, honey gland from attractive surface of lid; B, digestive gland from interior of pitcher, in pocket-like depression of epidermis (opening downwards); C, transverse section of the same.

of very large flask-shaped glands along the very edge of this incurved rim, and presumably of further attractiveness. The edges of the flutings are often produced downwards into stout hook-like processes, which are sometimes strong enough to retain a small bird.

Scraping our microscopic preparations as before, we may rapidly note the nectar-glands of the attractive lid, the flask-shaped marginal glands just referred to, the smooth internal conductive surface, and below this the secreting surface. The former often shows small downward-directed crescentic ledges, while when we come to the secreting surface we find these suddenly becoming better developed and crowded, each ridge bearing below it a well-developed gland, which projects slightly, like a watch just beginning to slip out of an inverted watch-pocket.

The fluid of the pitcher stands at a tolerably regular level, and so far as the insect visitors are concerned replaces the detentive surface of Sarracenia. That it is a normal and genuine secretion, and not mere collected rain, is evident from its development before the young pitcher has opened; while its analysis by Voelcker shows the presence of oxalic and citric acids, of chloride of potassium, and of carbonate of soda, magnesia, and lime. Lawson Tait again denies the presence of acid in the fluid of a young pitcher. Of much greater importance, however, is the interpretation of its nature and uses first promulgated by Sir Joseph Hooker in a memorable address to the British Association in 1874, in which he gave full details of his experiments on the digestive properties of the fluid, which he tested not only upon insects, morsels of beef, egg, etc., but even upon substances so resisting as cartilage. Lawson Tait in 1875, and subsequently Rees and Will of Erlangen in 1876: Gorup-Besanez, the well-known physiological chemist of Strasburg, in 1877; Vines, and others, confirmed these results, and extended them by the separation of a digestive ferment, apparently identical with the pepsin of the animal stomach. Rees and Will actually found that fibrin was dissolved even more rapidly by the secretion of the excited pitchers than in a test experiment with pepsin from the pig's stomach! This, it must be confessed, seems proving too much, and we shall do well to remember that most samples of prepared pepsin are far from possessing the same digestive potency, still less that of the fresh stomach, not to insist on other sources of fallacy. Still the existence of *some* appreciable quantity of pepsin seems obvious. Hooker and Tait have shown that fluid removed from a living pitcher into a glass vessel does not digest unless some acid, preferably lactic, be added. During the presence of food, however, they regard the pitcher as continuously stimulated to secrete acid, and to keep up the supply of pepsin.

Tait also separated a very deliquescent substance from the secretion of this and other insectivorous plants, which he termed *azerin*. To this he ascribed digestive and antiseptic properties, and also drew attention to its remarkable power of wetting surfaces, just as glycerine or paraffin does. Placing living flies in tubes containing distilled water, Nepenthes fluid, and solution of prepared azerin, he observed that " when those in the tube containing the water touch the surface they remain there as long as the water is undisturbed without ever getting completely wetted, and that they live for a very long time,—as long, perhaps, as in a perfectly dry tube. Those in the other tubes, on the contrary, will become completely wetted in a very few minutes after they touch the surface of the fluid, soon become immersed, and seldom live more than a quarter of an hour or twenty minutes."

"This must be due to the peculiar wetting property of azerin, enabling the water to enter their tracheæ and drowning them. This method of death can be seen in the case of flies placed upon the leaves of *Drosera rotundifolia*, for they become wetted in a way which was most astonishing to me until I knew the peculiar properties of azerin. In the process of digestion this penetration of the fluid must also be useful."

Secreting Glands as Nectaries.—So far we have been looking at the glands of the Nepenthes pitcher as peculiar organs special to their position; but soon after the re-examination of the pitcher by Professor Dickson, which resulted in the discovery of those curious marginal glands (which we may view as the highest specialisation of the gland structures of the lid and pitcher—perhaps, indeed, of the secreting gland yet known in the vegetable kingdom), Dr. Macfarlane made an interesting step towards the determination of the less specialised organ to which the whole of these peculiar structures may be referred, and of which they may be considered developments and modifications. Closely examining the whole plant, he noticed that "not only is honey secreted by the inside of the lid and the mouth of the pitcher, as we already knew, but the *outer* surface of the pitcher, as well as that of the lid, also possesses honey glands. Further, the whole so-called 'leaf,' or expanded lamina, including the thong-like prolongation of the midrib, to the end of which the pitcher is attached, may be regarded as a complete insect-lure, seeing it also is found to be studded with honey-secreting glands, thus presenting to unwary insects a long but pleasant passage to the cavity of the pitcher below. The stem, too, was found to possess glands for honey secretion—in some species to a greater extent than in others." The curator of the Edinburgh Botanic Garden drew Dr. Macfarlane's attention to the viscid nature of the fluid secreted by Nepenthes when flowering, and it was found that this also was a honey secretion, and glands were discovered to be present on the upper epidermis of the sepals. Dr. Macfarlane then made a minute examination of the other three genera of pitchered insectivorous plants at present in cultivation — viz. Sarracenia, Darlingtonia, and Cephalotus — with the result that substantially the same condition of things was found to subsist in them all. "The pitcher-plants may thus be regarded as ingenious mechanisms for first attracting insects, in order to receive their aid in fertilisation; and next, for the capture of these insects, and their subsequent appropriation for purposes of nutrition." These are in fact the "extra-floral nectaries" well known in many plants, and which the reader may most conveniently learn to know by looking for them on a shoot of cherry laurel.

CHAPTER II

PITCHER PLANTS — *continued*

Use of Pitchers, "Bionomics" — Bionomics — Bionomics of Nepenthes — Morphology of the Pitcher — Bladderwort — Bionomics of Bladderwort — Allied Forms.

Use of Pitchers, "Bionomics." — The view of the economy of the Nepenthes pitcher held more or less strongly by some older naturalists, that this was a benevolent provision of nature to comfort the weary traveller or refresh the thirsty bird, had of course given way; not so much before the distributional fact that these plants inhabit wet places in tropical forest thickets (where even if travellers were wont to pass, they with the birds would not need to seek so far for water), as from the general decay of this cheaply optimistic teleology. Yet so habitual was this way of looking at things that we have even had in more modern times the pitchers of Sarracenia and Darlingtonia described as caves of refuge supplied by a benevolent Providence to conceal insects from their pursuers.

Some better explanation was needed, and the new one, in terms of that grim and all-pervading struggle for existence, which naturalists were learning from Darwin and the times to substitute along the whole line for the old-fashioned "harmony of nature," could not but at once arrest attention and quickly win its way to acceptance and approval, the more so because of its new and dramatic form, the plant, usually the passive prey of the animal, turning the tables and making the animal its victim. A great step was thus made towards realising that view of nature, that physiology not of the machinery of the individual merely, but of species in their relation to all the life around them, which it is probably the very greatest of all Darwin's services to have put before us in so many of its scenes. This is what many old writers meant by "Natural History," and what too many modern German authors unfortunately confuse with the well-established general name including all the fields of organic science as "Biologie." Semper therefore prefers to speak of this his favourite study (see his *Animal Life* in International Science Series) as the "physiology of organisms," of course in distinction to the physiology of organs. Mr. Wallace terms this the "higher physiology," while Professor Ray Lankester has suggested the convenient term of bionomics.

The last term has many advantages, not the least being that its very sound and form helps us to realise its meaning as expressing the *economics* of each of the innumerable species with which we share the planet. It is, we trust, likely to come into general use, and to supersede the vague or confused terms above mentioned.

Bionomics. — It is important clearly to distinguish in the work and influence of Darwin the various elements; since putting aside altogether his evolutionary theories, his work in thus reopening the study of natural history in its widest aspects, of constituting *Bionomics* as Cuvier did Comparative Anatomy or Palæontology, or Linnæus Taxonomy, must always remain of the first magnitude. It is thus worth a little time fully to realise this. The child at first delightedly watches the bees and butterflies upon the flowers; grown a little older he hunts and kills; and by and by, when the civilised "mania of owning things" has arisen, he collects. At school and college he learns to name and to analyse; normally too, alas! to forget all discontent though grammar be substituted for literature, and form in all things for life, and though every outdoor aspect of nature be forgotten during a whole youth wasted in imprisonment between the whitewashed schoolroom and the ball exercise-yard of his school. Thus prepared, circumstances may make him "a naturalist" again, but now with a difference from his childish startingpoint. His first impulse will be to seek his accounts of nature in books and to comment on his predecessor, as naturalists did all through the middle ages, and as most of us do too much still; if he go beyond this it is in the first place to make a collection; especially as he has here the lucid logic, the consummate academic discipline handed on from Linnæus to guide him, and so he becomes a systematist—it may be a Bentham or an Agardh; but if so, concentrating himself on his herbarium, group by group, leaving the insects to their keeper over the way in the Zoological Museum. Or a later medical education (itself of course deeply influenced from the schools) may dominate the preliminary one, and thus we get an anatomist—it may be an Owen or a Huxley—and so far indeed our contemporary university and school presentation of natural science has now actually come—witness the accepted text-books (excellent of course from their point of view) of "Elementary Biology," "Practical Botany," and their various sources and imitations. But all this time we have been taking no sufficient note of Darwin. He, happiest as well as greatest of naturalists, has gone straight through school and college, but obviously with but an irreducible minimum of their result upon him. Still fresh from the gardens and woodlands of childish and boyish home, he passes to his

"Naturalist's Voyage." Year after year, he watches for himself the drama of organic nature, sees it more fully and more deeply than ever great naturalist before had the good hap to do; and so returns to use indeed the museum and the scalpel as well as another, but always as a mere means to an end—that of watching the organic drama, scene by scene, and if it might be deciphering the inner mechanism of the plot. For him, as for not a few penetrating predecessors, the plot is *Evolution* (whatever that may mean), and his special interpretation of its mechanism is his world-famous "theory of natural selection," at which we have already glanced, and to which we shall come more fully by and by. Now it is plain that this reading of the drama of the universe neither began with Darwin nor can end with him; it is indeed at the very outset frankly to be admitted as one of the purposes of this little book to help the reader towards getting beyond the Darwinian theory of the progress of nature; yet all the more must it be insisted on, not only that we appreciate clearly what that theory is,— and this, of course, in no mere literary fashion,—but as an actual seeing of nature, scene by scene, as it appeared to Darwin's eyes: this too not merely for the general theoretic interest, much less the special controversial one just hinted at, but for its intrinsic interest as well—indeed first and foremost. At the drama of evolution mankind are but awakening spectators; here is one who, even if we put aside his general interpretation of its nature and mechanism for the moment altogether, we should still have to appeal to as not only the most patient but the most penetrating of observers. We cannot have, it is true, too full a list of the kinds or "species" of the innumerable and strangely varied *dramatis personæ*; we cannot look too closely into their corpses as they fall, else we shall fail to understand much; if we dry or pickle these sad remains they will be of use for reference. Even more useful is it to excavate ancestral tombs, and bring out their fossils; indeed none has set us a better example than Darwin himself in all these very ways.

But not the smallest living scene — not even this bee upon its flower — is to be understood from our museums and herbaria: for this exhaustive division of labour, with its entomological and botanical specialists, in winning extension of exact and detailed special knowledge, had lost sight of developing that vague general knowledge with which childhood begins. Watching the bees among the flowers is an old and happy occupation, not only for children but their elders, and many a writer, from the prosaic economist up to the master of all poets, has long ago said his say; their points of view, however, were alike always too impressionist or too anthropomorphic in standpoint to contribute anything towards exact natural science, and so mummy-labelling and shelving went on indoors undisturbed. Once only a hundred years ago a childlike old German botanist went out into the garden and watched summer after summer, till he saw what the bees were doing, all unconsciously, to the flowers, and learned how they and the flowers were fitted one to the other in every detail of form like hand and glove; and when he was sure of his facts he could keep the secret no longer; he noted down everything that he had seen, and this too with excellent drawings, calling his book, in naïve childlike delight and pride, *The Secret of Nature Discovered!* But the botanists indoors would not look at his book, save at most to say — What nonsense! what childish fancies! what waste of time! So it was soon forgotten, and lay for a century unnoticed, until a naturalist, not conventionalised in the museums, nor over-educated for his intellect, but persistently childlike in questioning and watching, and watching and questioning again, should come once more. And so Darwin wrote *On the Fertilisation of Orchids*, and Hermann Müller, Hildebrand, Kerner, Delpino, followed suit; while MacLeod and a whole younger generation are following these nowadays.

Bionomics of Nepenthes.—It is time to return from the history of bionomics in general to our special scene; that of Nepenthes, luring and entrapping its flying and creeping insect prey. We may now group around this some of the minor incidents which naturalists have gradually described. Thus a recent traveller in Borneo descants upon the superior intelligence of certain ants, who refuse to be inveigled into the pitchers, and succeed in drinking its fluid contents, rich with the sapid juices of their less wary congeners, by piercing and sucking the tendril-like stalk upon which the pitcher hangs. He or another even credits them with knowing that water rises to its own level, and so with taking care not to pierce the stalk higher than the level of the fluid in the adjacent pitcher! It is a good story, and constructed on excellent, one may almost say standard, lines; the sceptical reader may wish, however, to know whether the ants, however, were not simply licking up the sugary exudation of those glands which, as above mentioned, were left to Dr. Macfarlane to notice outside the pitcher, and which, especially in a species so carefully treated by the ants, might fairly be expected to be more abundant as one descended towards it. Be this as it may, we owe to the same observer another interesting picture, that of the odd little lemur (*Tarsius spectrum*) prowling over the Nepenthes pitchers, fishing out with its long-clawed fingers their insect contents, and confiscating them to its own use. One species, however (*N. bicalcarata*), he tells us, gets the better of the Tarsius, repelling, and if need be punishing, the robber by help of a pair of long strong prickles which grow from the lower side of the base

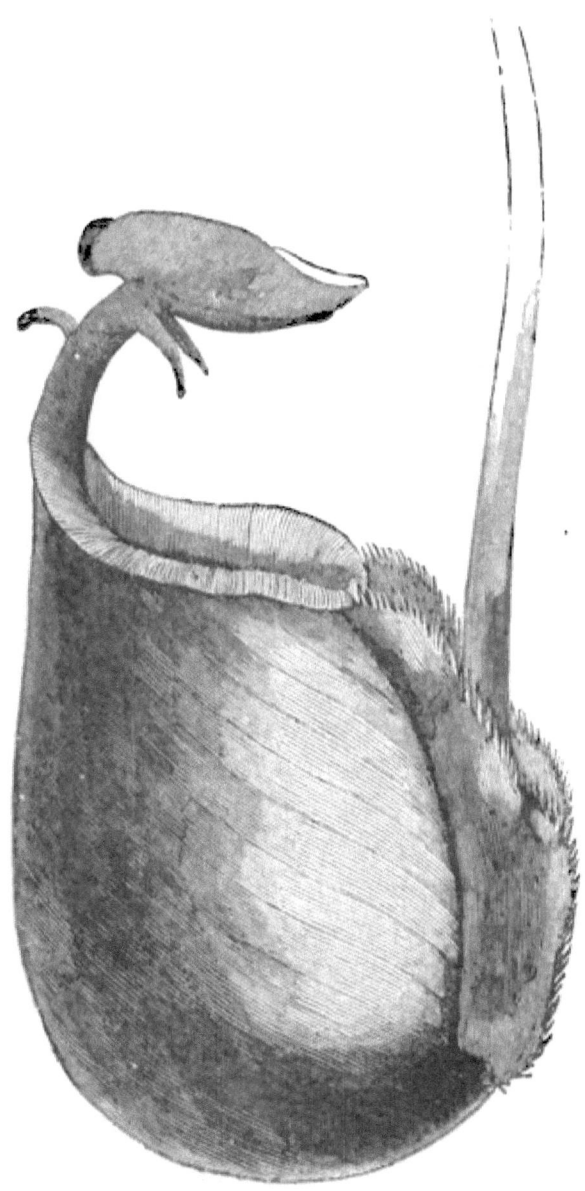

FIG. 4. — Pitcher of *Nepenthes bicalcarata* showing downward-directed prickles. (After Burbidge.)

of the lid downwards into the pitcher opening, their points ending just where the intruder would naturally insinuate its neck. And so on, as with Sarracenia, we see that nature's scenes are like Shakespearian ones: around the main incident (or what we take to be that) there may be grouped all manner of by-play, here quaint or picturesque, or again laden with deadly issues.

Morphology of the Pitcher. — Baillon, and indeed first of all Linnæus, pointed out that by exaggerating the concavity of a (peltate) leaf like that of the Water-lily (*Nymphæa*) we might obtain a pitcher like that of Sarracenia. Baillon has described intermediate forms — incipient pitchers — exhibited by a variety of *Peperomia arifolia*, a plant allied to the Peppers, and without going so far afield we may see exhibited nearly every year at meetings of botanical or horticultural societies specimens of monstrous pitcher leaves in cabbage, lime, and other plants, where elongated stalk or enrolled leaf forms a well for the raindrops. A recent writer describes such a pitcher upon a leaf of vetch (*Vicia sepium*), of which he ascribes the origin to the puncture of an insect.

Heckel's theory of the pitcher of Sarracenia is that it represents a hollowed leaf-stalk, the lid corresponding to the blade of the leaf. However this may be, the interpretation already given of the Darlingtonia pitcher as a further development of that of Sarracenia of course remains unaltered.

Many authors have been wont to regard the broad leafy portion of the Nepenthes as but a marginal expansion of the lower portion of the leaf-stalk, the tendril being its upper portion, and the pitcher thus corresponding to the whole leaf, pouched as we have seen is actually the case in Cephalotus. They trace the margins of the leaf in its external wings, and point out the little threadlike tip of the leaf just behind the lid.

For Hooker the tendril is a simple prolongation of the leaf such as we see in various leaves, *e.g.* the lily-climber *Gloriosa*, while he describes the development of the pitcher as a simple dimpling and deepening of the upper surface near the extreme tip of the tendril, which survives as the mere rudiment already mentioned. He explains this strange development as finding its possible initial rudiment in those water-secreting glands common at the tip of so many leaves, an apparatus which the reader may see at work in the drop which often hangs at the leaf tip of his white "Lily of the Nile" (*Richardia africana*); still better, in many greenhouse arums; or, best of all, on the dew-gemmed leaves of Lady's Mantle (*Alchemilla vulgaris*) in a summer morning's walk. Applying our histological experience, too, we may prepare excellent microscopic specimens of these water glands from the leaf tips of Saxifrages or of Indian Cress (*Tropæolum*) by carefully scraping away the lower epidermis and parenchyma upon a glass slide in a drop of water, and then turning over the remaining epidermis to show its upper surface.

Partly from his study of the pitcher leaves of seedling Nepenthes, which appear immediately after the cotyledons, and in which the pitcher seemed to him to develop from the first as a much more important portion of the leaf, Dickson was led to give up this doctrine of Hooker's. The curiously "interrupted" leaves of some Crotons (*C. interruptus*), in which the flat portion, the intervening midrib, and even the pitcher in a rudimentary form, are all present, the latter as simply the upper third of the leaf, seemed to him to afford the key to the difficulty; the detailed development of the pitcher as a leaf pouching seeming to him essentially similar to that of Cephalotus, above mentioned. Dr. Macfarlane's conclusions as to the nature of the pitchers are very different. He believes that in Nepenthes, Heliamphora, Sarracenia, and Darlingtonia alike, the pitcher is developed from what is originally a compound leaf, consisting of from two to five pairs of leaflets. But there is a marked tendency to dorsal fusion of these leaflets from apex to base. Such fused leaflets are seen in the broad basal part of the Nepenthes leaf, and in the flaps and lids of the various pitchers. The pitcher itself is a deep dorsal involution of the midrib just above the termination of the fused upper pair of leaflets, except, indeed, in Cephalotus, where, as Dickson clearly showed, it is an involution of the leaf blade.

Professor Bower by no means agrees with Macfarlane. He interprets the lid of Nepenthes as composed of a single pair of leaflets fused together; on the other hand, the lid of Sarracenia as merely the flattened terminal portion of the modified leaf.

Gœbel lays stress upon the scantiness of the evidence upon which both these ingenious rival theories of the complex origin of the pitcher have been erected, and believes that the structure of all the pitchers is very much the same, that all may be derived from a peltate leaf in which a deep involution of the upper surface has occurred. As to the side wings, in which some see the vestiges of leaflets, he regards them as entirely secondary growths.

We have cited all these opinions — and we might have given others — just because in their puzzling divergence they illustrate the difficulty, yet fascination, of morphological studies. It is not important to the student to "get up" this doctrine or that; indeed the teacher may with advantage postpone or even refrain altogether from expressing his own judgment; what really is important is that the student should know how such a question is asked and answered — partly by a study of the actual form alike in its obvious and in its microscopic structure; partly by comparing the form in question with that of nearly related plants; partly by observation of the young plants and their gradual development; partly by attention to those monstrosities which often reveal the secret of strange structures. It is only when the student has learned to place himself at the standpoint of several distinct theories, and to state and weigh these impartially, that he becomes able to give his adherence to one or other view. Nor can he fully do this without reading for himself the original papers, and perhaps reinvestigating the subject for himself after all.

Bladderwort.—Our tour round the world in search of pitcher-plants may find appropriate completion in the discovery of one not less interesting almost at our own doors. In marshy lochs and mountain tarns the Common Bladderwort makes itself conspicuous for a month or two in summer, when from the floating stem the flower-stalk rises bearing quaint bright golden blossoms, somewhat orchid-like in appearance, though really akin to the primroses, which are commonly considered to represent the simpler regular ancestral form, much as do lilies to orchids, or potato-blossom to foxgloves and snapdragon. At other times the plant is not so readily seen, for it floats in the water, and its leaves are small. Like some other aquatic plants the water bladderworts have no roots, and the straggling stem bears numerous, much-divided slender leaves. Among these are hundreds of little bladders. From the main submerged stem of *Utricularia vulgaris*, and yet more markedly in tropical species, peculiar thin shoots, which Gœbel calls "aerial shoots," rise to the surface, and bear leaves slightly different from those on the other parts of the stem. It seems likely that this part of the plant is of special use in effecting interchange of gases with the air.

Each bladder—shown by its mode of development to be

a modified leaflet — is a simple but effective trap. It is a hollow chamber, about $\frac{1}{10}$ of an inch in length, entered by a thin transparent door or valve which opens inwards only and allows of no egress, for it shuts instantly, as if with a spring, against an anterior thickened collar or projection around the mouth.

These traps are very fatal to small Crustaceans, popularly known as water-fleas, which swarm in every freshwater basin. Pursued by their enemies, or attracted perhaps by a slight mucilage which is exuded from glands on the door of the trap, or prompted it may be by wayward curiosity, the water-fleas clamber on six or seven long stiff bristle-like processes which project from the mouth of the bladder. So far they are safe enough, but if they explore farther, and push before them the inward-yielding door of the bladder, they are within a prison from which there is no escape. For a day or two they may live, but the trap becomes crowded with prisoners, and they die. No digestion occurs, but the bodies of the animals are decomposed by Bacteria, and the products of decomposition are absorbed. That these products are useful to the bladderwort is confirmed by Büsgen's observation that those plants from which all water-fleas were artificially excluded did not flourish so well as those in normal conditions. Darwin believed that the four-fold hairs which occur abundantly over the internal surface of the bladder were absorbent structures, but this is by no means certain. Indeed these peculiar hairs are connected by intermediate forms with the slime-secreting hairs found outside the bladders, for instance on the door. It is worth noting that such hairs are to be found in many aquatic plants quite innocent of insect catching; as, for instance, on the leaves of *Callitriche verna*. Chodat, and after him others, have shown that they arise from cells which under ordinary circumstances would have formed the stomata of an aerial leaf. (See Chap. IX.)

The seasonal life of the aquatic bladderwort is interesting. Throughout the summer it floats on the surface of the water, and the straggling stem grows at one end as it dies away at the other. Perhaps too many decomposing Crustaceans, however good for the growth of the plant, may not be altogether good for the leaves which most directly receive this liberal manuring. As the summer ends, and as the water-fleas cease to swarm in the pond, the life of the plant becomes concentrated in a thick-set terminal tuft. This, as in some other aquatic plants, sinks to the bottom of the pond and passes the winter there. In spring, lightened perhaps of what stores of reserve material it contained, the stem rises again, and forming a fresh set of bladders begins to grow vigorously at the surface. The older botanists, *e.g.* A. P. de Candolle, believed that the bladders were floats for the plants; at first they were filled with mucus, and the plant rested at the bottom; afterwards they were filled with gas, and the plant rose to the surface. This was a pretty notion, but not true. The plant will float without any bladders, or when all are full of water; the bladders have really nothing to do with the floating.

Bionomics of Bladderwort. — It may be that the water-fleas enter the bladders in search of Infusorians and other small creatures on which they feed; it seems likely, too, that the bladderwort does really profit by the capture of the water-fleas. There is another strand in the web. Amid the Utricularia one commonly finds certain water-spiders, who make for themselves a diving-bell with air which they carry from the surface, their bubble glistening like silver as they descend. Have not these clever creatures come to recognise that the bladders of Utricularia are so many larders, and do not they rifle them? Thus, as in former cases, there would be a play within a play.

Allied Forms.—Not all the species of Utricularia, however, are aquatic; some, especially in the Tropics, are terrestrial plants. In these, though the booty is of course different, the bladders sometimes borne by the creeping underground stems may capture small terrestrial animals, larval earthworms, centipedes, and the like, much in the same way as the aquatic species do. The same is true of an allied terrestrial genus (Polypompholix). The terrestrial bladderworts usually live in damp places, but some are perched on the mossy stems of trees. For each kind of habitat there are special adaptations: the aquatic forms have sometimes air-reservoirs which act as buoys for the upright flower-stalk; the epiphytes often have water-reservoirs which enable them to survive the dry season; the terrestrial species, though rootless like all the others, have little processes or rhizoids which descend into the ground, especially at the base of the flower-stalk, and serve to steady the latter as well as to absorb water.

Allied to the Utricularia there is another rarer insectivorous plant, Genlisea, which is represented by several species from Brazil, Cuba, and Angola. It lives in marshy places, and, like the bladderwort, is rootless. The stem rises upright from the ground, and is thickly beset with leaves, most of which are spathulate, while others are modified into strange twisted descending staircases. These are long-necked and lined with downward-directed hairs, which at once aid an animal in its entrance and prevent its retreat.

Pinguicula, Utricularia, and Genlisea all belong to the same order (Lentibulariaceæ), and may be grouped, as Gœbel points out, in a series. "We regard," he says, "forms like Pinguicula with a rosette of slimy leaves and a central flower-stalk as near the starting-point of the series. From this Genlisea has diverged in one direction, Utricularia in another. That they have lost their roots is not to be wondered at, for they are in great part aquatic plants. Genlisea diverges but little from the hypothetical ancestral form; it has indeed very remarkable bladders, but it retains the rosette of leaves seen in Pinguicula. This is still represented in the terrestrial bladderworts, but here there are most marvellous modifications of leaves which obliterate the distinctions between leaf and shoot. In the aquatic bladderworts the terminal floral axis of the seedling is suppressed, but there is still a rosette of leaves, though often only in rudimentary form. The strength of the development lies in the floating shoots, which are homologous with leaves."

Before we leave the pitcher-plants and bladderworts, we shall simply notice another strange plant — the Scaly Toothwort (*Lathræa squamaria*), which is sometimes found in our woods. It is a parasite on the roots of trees and shrubs, and being without chlorophyll looks wan and strange. We shall return to it in a subsequent chapter, but it is of interest here to notice that its underground toothlike leaves are not only solidly thickened stores for the food-reserve appropriated from their hosts, but contain small hollow traps in which many kinds of small terrestrial animals are ensnared. The underground buds of *Bartsia alpina* show a somewhat similar structure, and also imprison minute animals. It is interesting also to note that these Bartsias with some of their nearest allies, like the pretty euphrasy and the curious yellow rattles and louseworts,[1] and one or two others, are all parasites upon other plants as well, their roots sucking those of grasses; while through them, as we shall see later, we pass to true parasites.

[1] *Euphrasia officinalis, Rhinanthus Crista-galli, Pedicularis sylvatica,* and *P. palustris.*

CHAPTER III

OTHER INSECTIVOROUS PLANTS — DIFFICULTIES AND CRITICISMS

Fly-Traps (Dionæa and Aldrovanda) — Sundews and Birdlime Traps — Butterworts — Sundews proper (Drosera) — Details, Functional and Structural — Digestion — Movements — Absorption — Utility — Other Insectivorous Plants — Legends — Difficulties — Further Difficulties and Criticisms — Direction of further Investigation; Possible Compromise.

Fly-Traps (Dionæa). — Besides those insectivorous plants which we have already studied under the general title of "pitchers," there are others more active in insect-catching, which we may call "fly-traps." Of these the most famous, cynically nicknamed "Venus's Fly-Trap" (*Dionæa muscipula*), grows in damp places in the east of North America, occurring in very local distribution in North and South Carolina, especially near the town of Wilmington. It was the first of the insectivorous plants to attract attention, for in 1768 Ellis, a London merchant, but a shrewd naturalist withal, who discerned the animal nature of coral, sent a description of the plant to Linnæus, who in his enthusiasm called it "*miraculum naturæ*." But he supposed that the insects were captured accidentally, and subsequently allowed to escape.

The Venus Fly-Trap, like its allies the Sundews, grows on the wet moorland. A circle of more or less prostrate leaves surrounds the base of a flower-stalk which bears numerous flowers at a height of four to six inches from the ground. Each leaf is a fly-trap. The broadly flattened or winged (*spathulate*) stalk is constricted to the midrib at its junction with the bilobed blade, the halves of which are movable on one another along the middle, closing together with a snap, as a very tightly-bound book will sometimes do. Around each margin are twelve to twenty long teeth, and, when the leaf closes, those of one side interlock with those of the other, thus forming a very perfect miniature rat-trap. The centre of each half-leaf bears numerous rosy glands, and on each side there are three hairs, which an old naturalist described as spikes to impale the captured insect, but which are really quite weak, and bend flat on a basal joint when the leaf closes.

The student will find it easy and useful to make a paper model, cutting it out the proper shape, folding it along the middle line, carefully fashioning the teeth at each margin, so as to interlock neatly, and gumming on the three hairs on each half-blade, or more simply snipping them from the texture of the paper. The glands may easily be supplied with a red pencil, and a toy, not to be despised by young or old, is the result. Let us see how the trap works. If we go — preferably on a warm and bright day — to our plant, which is common in greenhouses in this country, and with a finger touch the leaf the closure follows. More careful experiment with anything nearer the size of the insect's leg, say a pencil-point, shows that we may wander all over both surfaces of the leaf or the marginal tentacles with safety until we touch one or more of the projecting hairs; and repeated experiment shows them to be alone sensitive — the two halves of the blade close. In the plant's native haunts some insect does what our finger did, and if in the rapid closure of the leaf the prey be caught, a secretion from the rosy glands immediately follows, and the leaf remains closed for a week or two according to the size of the insect. During that time the leaf acts as a temporary stomach, and the insect is digested and absorbed, as far at least as can be expected, and then the leaf reopens, but remains for a time in a torpid state. Sometimes, however, if the insect caught happen to be a very large one, the leaf never opens again, its meal proving too much for it; and even in a state of nature the most vigorous leaves are rarely able to digest more than twice, or at most thrice, during their life.

The attractive rosy patches on the leaf, the rapid closure of the blade on its midrib, the interlocking of the teeth around the margin, the specialised sensitiveness of the six jointed hairs, the copious secretion of the digestive glands, combine to make Dionæa a very efficient fly-trap.

The secretion poured out from the stimulated glands contains formic acid and a digestive ferment. It further resembles gastric juice in having marked antiseptic qualities; thus when Lindsay fed leaves with such quantities of meat as to kill them with indigestion, the meat inside remained fresh while portions hanging outside putrefied. So abundant is the secretion that when Darwin made a small opening at the base of one lobe of a leaf which had closed over a large crushed fly, the secretion continued to run down the footstalk during the whole time — nine days — during which the plant was kept under observation. That absorption follows digestion is shown by the disappearance of the digestible substances, and Fraustadt was able, by feeding leaves with albumen stained with aniline red, to colour the contents and nuclei of the gland-cells.

The three pairs of hairs are exquisitely sensitive to the contact of solid bodies, but are indifferent to wind and rain. The triangular area between the bases of the hairs is slightly sensitive, and if the general surface of the leaf be wounded closure may occur. Inorganic or non-nitrogenous bodies placed on the leaves without touching the hairs do not excite any movement, but nitrogenous substances, if in the least degree damp, cause after several hours the lobes to close slowly. Leaves which have made a mistake and have closed over useless bodies, reopen after a few hours, or at most a day's rest, and are again ready for action. According to Macfarlane, mechanical stimulus of the fly-trap requires two touches, unless the stimulus be very powerful, and the touches must be separated by an interval greater than one-third of a second. If less than one-third of a second be allowed as interval, no contraction follows, and a third touch is then necessary.

As to the movement of the fly-trap. Darwin detected a measurable contraction or alteration of form, and showed that the movement follows a stimulus passing through the cellular tissue from the sensitive hairs. There are really two kinds of movement — one rapid, which follows the irritation of the sensitive hairs; the other slow, excited chemically, as when the leaves gradually tighten their hold on a fly and bring the glands on both sides into contact with it. Burdon Sanderson shows that the electrical conditions associated with the rest and activity of the leaf are closely like those observed in our muscles. Not only is there a normal electric current in the leaf, but at the moment of closure there is what animal physiologists know as a "negative variation," due to the conversion of electromotive force into mechanical work. These facts lead us to believe with Burdon Sanderson that "the property by virtue of which the excitable structures of the leaf respond to stimulation is of the same nature as that possessed by the similarly endowed structures of animals."

Aldrovanda. — Allied to Dionæa, and with a somewhat similar leaf, is a water fly-trap (*Aldrovanda vesiculosa*), which lives in clear well-sunned ponds in south and central Europe, and also occurs in Australia and India. Like the common bladderwort, Aldrovanda has a thin rootless floating stem, which bears whorls of modified leaves. It dies away at one end as it grows at the other, and is reduced in autumn to a concentrated tuft, which sinks for the winter to the muddy bottom of the pond, thence to rise again in summer after it has exhausted its stores of starch and has become buoyant with gas. The little leaves have a spathulate stalk and a folding two-lobed blade with teeth round the edges. Although in figures of the plant the leaves are commonly represented as open, like those of Dionæa, it is said that their lobes really open only about as much as the valves of a living mussel, and are thus the better fitted for capturing small animals. The surface bears numerous sensitive jointed hairs and colourless stalked glands, and the leaf closes on water-fleas, larvæ of insects, and even diatoms, very much after the fashion of Dionæa. Darwin believed that the glands secrete a digestive fluid, and that small four-lobed hairs situated on the outer thinner parts of the leaf absorb decaying animal matter. Gœbel is inclined to think that these four-lobed hairs secrete some slimy substance, perhaps attractive to small animals.

Sundews and Birdlime Traps. — It is said that Portuguese peasants use as a substitute for fly-paper the viscid leaves of *Drosophyllum lusitanicum*, a common plant in dry, sandy, or rocky places in Portugal and Morocco, and hence, it is worth noting, with a much better developed root system than its marsh-loving allies. It grows eight or ten inches high, and has long narrow strap-like leaves (which are interesting as being rolled up in the bud like those of ferns, but backwards instead of forwards), beset with stalked glands which secrete a viscid dewdrop-like juice. On these leaves insects, attracted it may be by the glistening drops and by the reddish colour, but more probably by the honey-like fragrance, alight, and knocking off drops from the stalked glands become besmeared and choked. They sink on the surface of the leaf and then small unstalked, uncoloured glands exude a dissolvent secretion. On a plant a year old, which had lived in a glass house with open doors, Gœbel on one occasion counted no less than 233 distinctly visible flies, distributed over nineteen leaves.

Belonging to the same order as Drosophyllum and the more familiar Drosera, there are two other sticky plants in which the "insectivorous habit" is not more than incipient. These are *Roridula dentata* from the Cape, and *Byblis gigantea*, the latter with simple glands, scarce differing appreciably from those on many other kinds of plants, though with a more copious and glutinous juice. They are interesting in showing the beginnings of the peculiarity which becomes so marked in the sundews, and in the same connection we should notice that leaves and stems of some geraniums, sedums, and primulas have glandular surfaces on which insects become entangled.

Butterworts. — The Common Butterwort (*Pinguicula vulgaris*) is very common on marshy grounds, especially among the hills. It has a wide geographical distribution, represents a genus with about forty species, and belongs to the same order as Utricularia (*Lentibulariaceæ*). It has long been known, though not in connection with insect-catching, for Linnæus noted that the Lapps used it for curdling milk. Every one who has tramped over high wet moorlands or followed the banks of a mountain stream up into the hills knows the appearance of the plant, — the rosette of plump glistening leaves prostrate on the ground, the beautiful violet flower raised on an upright stalk. The plump leaves, to which the plant owes its quaint name Pinguicula (= little fat one), have a characteristic fungus-like smell perhaps attractive, and are covered with stalked and unstalked glands, which exude a copious viscid secretion. This obviously catches insects, and further, Darwin tells us, also digests the small flies and midges which carelessly allow themselves to be limed. To the touch of other things, raindrops or sand-grains for instance, the butterwort is indifferent, but a little insect provokes abundant secretion. But this is not all; the leaf moves, slightly capable of motion as it seems. When an insect is entangled, the edges of the leaf curl slowly inwards for an hour or two, not fast enough indeed to catch an insect, but that is not necessary, yet sufficiently to enclose the booty, or shift it inwards, or at least expose it to the action of a greater number of glands. The result is that the insect's body is soon dissolved away, only indigestible chitinous shreds being left.

It seems that the butterwort forms the two ferments of most gastric juice — a rennet-like ferment, to which the plant's power of curdling milk is due; and a digestive or peptic ferment, which dissolves the usable parts of the bodies of insects. It is possible that the antiseptic properties of these ferments justify the old custom of applying the leaves of the butterwort to the sores of cattle, but we should not like to commit ourselves to any such apology, since the coolness and dampness of such a plaster and its special power of keeping flies from the sores are evidently so far sufficient.

Professor J. R. Green describes a rennet-forming ferment comparable to that of the calf's stomach — not only in Pinguicula, but in the flowers of the yellow bedstraw (*Galium verum*), in the stem of the Clematis, in the petals of the Artichoke, and in other plants. A peptonising ferment, like that of the gastric juice, occurs not only in insectivorous plants, but in situations so different as the seeds of the Vetch or the milky juice of the papaw-tree (*Carica papaya*). In warm countries, where of course fresh meat cannot be hung for any length of time, it is common to make a joint rapidly tender by applying to it the leaves of this tree, a practice which probably finds its explanation in this presence of ferment. There is also in some plants an emulsifying and saponifying ferment, which acts on fats and oils as the juice of the animal pancreas does; while the diastase, which, as in germinating malt, turns starch into sugar, is closely comparable to the ferment of the salivary juice in animals.

Although from our present physiological standpoint we have delayed mention of the butterwort until coming to the sundews, its structural relations are with the bladderworts and Genlisea. This is shown not only by the characters of the flower, but in minute details, for, according to Gœbel, the two sets of glands in Pinguicula and the slime-secreting hairs of Utricularia and Genlisea are all fundamentally the same.

Sundews proper (Drosera).—Beside the butterwort on the marshy moor, we may perhaps find one of the Sundews (Drosera). The genus is a large one, and the species are widely distributed over the northern parts of both hemispheres. In almost all countries and languages they bear the same pretty and, so far as description goes, appropriate name—*Rossolis, Sonnentau,* Sundew.

Our commoner British species—*Drosera rotundifolia*—grows loosely rooted in marshy and peaty ground, often embedded among the bog-moss which forms a fitting background for the rich red colour of the leaves. These, to the number of half a dozen or so, lie prostrate, and from their midst arises a small upright stalk with inconspicuous whitish flowers. Each leaf consists of a long narrow stalk, expanded into a more or less circular blade, the edges and surface of which bear scores of club-like "hairs" or "tentacles," apparently tipped with dew. These hairs are complex structures; the head of each is glandular and well supplied with water-pipes (spirally thickened wood-fibres or "tracheides"); it is the viscid secretion of the gland which makes the apparent dewdrop.

These hairs or tentacles, then, are sensitive, mobile, digestive, and absorptive — most marvellous little structures, indifferent to the drops of rain which often fall upon them, but responsive to the stimulus of a midge. An insect unwary or deluded alights on the leaf, and is forthwith entangled; as it struggles the secretion becomes more abundant. The tentacles too bend down upon the entangled midge; first one, and in a few minutes another, and another, till all the two hundred may close upon the prey like so many slow merciless fingers. The leaf may become more concave, and after complete closure looks like a closed fist. As the result of the secretion the booty is digested and the products of digestion absorbed.

So far the usual general description of the sundew; but now let us take up Darwin's *Insectivorous Plants*, and read up the details, for there is no more characteristic example of his patient elaborate way of working than his account of the sundew.

Further Details of Functional or Structural Interest. — There are on an average about two hundred glandular tentacles. The stalk of each has the essential structure of a leaf: a small "fibro-vascular bundle," consisting mainly of spiral tracheides, runs up the centre, and is surrounded by a layer of elongated cells lined by a thin layer of colourless circulating protoplasm, and filled with a purplish fluid. The glandular head of the tentacle contains a central mass of spirally thickened cells in immediate contact with the upper ends of the conducting tracheides. Around these, but separated from them by an intermediate stratum of elongated cells, there is a layer of cells filled with purple fluid, and outside these another somewhat similar layer. These two external layers form the really glandular part. Gœbel insists that all the glands of Droseraceæ, whether borne on tentacles, as in the common sundews, or quite unstalked, as in Dionæa, have essentially the same structure; the tentacled and the sessile forms are connected by intermediate gradations.

The leaves of the sundew seem to have some fascination for insects, but whether this is due to their colour, their glittering secretion, their odour, or to all three, remains uncertain. The drops are so viscid that an insect may be caught if it but touch one or two of the outer tentacles; as they begin to bend and also secrete more copiously the insect is carried inwards and more effectively smeared. Even a large insect — such as a dragon fly — may be caught by several leaves, though in these cases it is likely that the insect was to begin with in a weak state. The bending of the tentacle takes place near its base, and may be excited in various ways. For although the plant seems to have grown accustomed to gusts of wind or drops of rain, and is to its own advantage indifferent to these, repeated touches will cause the tentacles to bend. On the other hand, contact with any solid particle, even though insoluble and of far greater minuteness than could be appreciated by our sense of touch, will induce movement, and one would think that in natural conditions movements so induced must sometimes occur, and to no purpose. A morsel of human hair, weighing only $\frac{1}{78740}$ of a grain, and this largely supported too by the viscid secretion, suffices to induce movement. Finally, the absorption of even a minute trace of certain fluids, especially nitrogenous, acts as a stimulus.

During the bending of the tentacle the secretion of the gland becomes more copious, and its chemical reaction changes from neutral to acid. Meantime within the stalk of the stimulated tentacle a strange change occurs, marked externally by a somewhat mottled appearance. When examined under the microscope the formerly homogeneous fluid contents of the cells of the stalk are seen to have separated in purple bead-like masses, of constantly varying number, shape, and size, and suspended in a colourless fluid. This change makes the layer of colourless circulating protoplasm which lines the cells more distinctly visible.

Darwin attached considerable importance to this process, which he termed "aggregation of the protoplasm." It begins in the glands, and gradually travels down the tentacle from cell to cell. After the action of the tentacle is over, a reverse process of redissolution of the protoplasm proceeds from the base upwards. Darwin believed that it was a vital process, only exhibited when the cells were alive and normal, not necessarily connected with either bending or increased secretion, and quite different from "plasmolysis" or the shrinking of the protoplasm from the cell-wall, which is observed when parts of plants are examined in any dense fluid which induces osmosis. Darwin observed a similar aggregation in the sensitive hairs of Dionæa, and in the roots of various plants, and believed that it was of wide occurrence and of profound importance in the physiology of the vegetable cell.

In connection with the sensitiveness of the Drosera, one of the most interesting of Darwin's observations was in regard to the salts of ammonia. All the salts of ammonia cause the tentacles to bend — the carbonate strongly, the nitrate even more so, and the phosphate most of all. But the remarkable fact is the sensitiveness of the tentacles to infinitesimal quantities. Thus the immersion of a leaf in a solution of the last-mentioned salt, so weak that each gland could absorb only about $\frac{1}{20000000}$ of a grain, is sufficient to produce complete inflection of the tentacles. Though the particles of solid matter which stimulate the olfactory nerves of animals, and so produce the sensation of smell in animals, must be very much smaller than this, as Mr. Darwin remarked, the fact remains truly wonderful that the absorption of so minute a quantity by a gland should induce some change in it, which leads to the transmission of a motor impulse down the entire length of the tentacle, causing the whole mass to bend, often through an angle of more than 180°, and this too in the absence of any specialised nervous system.

It is not much to our present purpose to discuss the numerous experiments which Darwin made on the action of salts and acids, drugs and poisons on the leaves of the sundew; but the effects of organic fluids are important. Darwin treated sixty-one leaves of Drosera with non-nitrogenous solutions — gum-arabic, sugar, starch, dilute alcohol, olive-oil, tea. The tentacles were not in a single case inflected. He then applied to sixty-four other leaves various nitrogenous fluids (milk, wine, albumen, infusion of meat, mucus, saliva, isinglass), and sixty-three had the tentacles and often the blades well inflected. Finally, taking twenty-three of the leaves which had served for the first experiment, and treating them with bits of meat or drops of nitrogenous fluids, all save a few, — apparently injured by exosmose caused by the density of the former solution of gum, sugar, etc., — were distinctly inflected.

Digestion. — That the sundew possesses power of digesting the insects which it catches is evidenced in great detail.

The secretion of the glands, like the gastric juice of animals, contains a digestive ferment and several acids, as Frankland, Rees and Will, Lawson Tait, and others have shown. But this is corroborated by what happens to little pieces of organic material placed upon the leaves. Darwin fed numerous plants with roast meat and minute cubes of boiled white of egg, and by way of check placed similar cubes in wet moss. Those in the moss putrefied, while those on the sundew were dissolved. Pollen-grains had their protoplasmic contents dissolved, and seeds were usually killed. It is interesting to notice further that the secretion obtained from tentacles stimulated by fragments of glass was not able to digest, showing that the ferment is not secreted until the glands have absorbed a trace of animal matter. Moreover, while the leaves were able to digest beef, egg, cheese, and the like, they could not digest horn, chitin, cellulose, and other such substances — thus completing the analogy with the gastric digestion of animals.

Movements. — As to the movements of the tentacles, experiments showed that pricking the leaf or the leaf-stalk did not induce any response, that the stalks of the glands were not stimulated by food, that in fact the glands alone were sensitive. When a tentacle receives an impulse either from its own gland or from the central tentacles, it bends towards the middle of the leaf, the short tentacles on which do not bend at all; in all other cases all the tentacles, even those of the centre, bend towards the point whence the stimulous comes. Thus all the tentacles of a leaf may be made to converge into two symmetrical groups by placing a fragment of phosphate of ammonia in the middle of each half of the blade.

Vivisection showed that the motor impulse travels through the cellular tissue, and not through the fibro-vascular bundles. An impulse thus travels more rapidly along than across the leaf, since from the shape and lie of the cells, fewer cell-walls have to be crossed in a given distance. When the central glands are stimulated they send some influence outwards, which reaches the external tentacles and glands. There we can see one of the results of its arrival in the process of aggregation which descends the tentacles.

To explain the actual mechanism of bending is a most difficult problem. Various suppositions have been made. Thus if we suppose the cells at the base of the tentacle to be in a state of high-water tension and to possess great elasticity, a rapid outflow of water might cause shrinkage and bending. Or it may be that the living matter of cells is contractile, like that of muscles. What then causes the outflow, *i.e.* how does the stimulous set it up? What meaning, again, are we to give to the "protoplasmic continuity," which has been traced between the living matter of cell and cell, and how far shall we grant a share in the matter to the contractility of this living network? And so we are face to face once more with perplexities to muse over; which, as they take form in definite questions, will lead the reader towards the larger treatises and to new reflection beyond their scope in turn.

Absorption.—It is difficult to make precise statements in regard to the plant's power of absorbing the digested substances. Clark fed Drosera with flies soaked in chloride of lithium, and after several days found that all parts of the plants when burned showed the characteristic spectrum of lithium. But this did not conclusively prove more than that the lithium salt had been absorbed by the plant. Lawson Tait, by cultivating plants with roots cut off and leaves buried in pure sand watered with an ammoniacal solution, showed that the sundew can not only absorb nutriment from its leaves, but can actually thrive by their aid alone, if supplied with a little nitrogenous material. Bennett described, not only in Drosera, but also in Dionæa and Nepenthes, what he termed "absorptive glands" lying beneath the epidermis, and sometimes furnished with papillæ, which rise above the surface.

Utility.—Relatively complete as Darwin's study of Drosera and other insectivorous plants was, it did not adequately meet the scepticism of those who doubted the utility of the habit. Though Knight in 1818 had thought that plants of Dionæa which he fed with morsels of beef throve better than others not so treated, many observers have since failed to see any improvement on insectivorous plants when regularly fed, or any disadvantage when prevented from obtaining animal food altogether. And others have gone so far as to assert that animal food was hurtful, having injured or killed their plants by feeding.

But it is obviously hazardous to draw conclusions as to the utility of the insectivorous habit from plants under cultivation. For it may be that plants living in the greenhouse have a richer supply of nitrogenous food from their roots than they can in natural conditions secure. Sundew and butterwort very often grow among bog-moss on the moors, hardly rooted, and therefore less adapted than ordinary plants to absorb nitrogenous salts from their soil, even supposing that these were present in abundance; which, it is worth noting, recent analyses of boggy soils show they are not. Here indeed may be the grounds of a fresh argument, since this relative scantiness of nitrogenous supplies in the natural surroundings of insectivorous plants may render them in part dependent on their peculiar animal diet.

Again, although it has often been noticed that a leaf of sundew or fly-trap may suffer, or even die, from the effects of too large a meal, this can hardly be regarded as a serious objection against the alleged utility of the insectivorous habit until we learn that the casualty is common in nature. A similar objection might indeed be urged against eating dinner.

The gap left in Darwin's work was soon filled by his son. Francis Darwin took six plates full of thriving plants of sundew, and divided off each by a transverse bar. Then, choosing the least flourishing side of each, he placed, on 12th June 1877, roast meat in morsels of about $\frac{1}{50}$ of a grain on the leaves, and renewed the dose at intervals. Soon the plants on the fed sides were clearly greener than those on the starved sides, and their leaves contained more chlorophyll and starch. In less than two months the number of flower-stalks was half as numerous again on the fed as on the unfed sides, while the number and diameter of the leaves and the colour of the flower-stalks all showed a great superiority. "The flower-stalks were all cut at the end of August, when their numbers were as 165 to 100, their total weight as 230 to 100, and the average weight per stem as 140 to 100 for the fed and unfed sides respectively. The total numbers of seed capsules were as 194 to 100, or nearly double, and the average number of seeds in each capsule as 12 to 10 respectively. The superiority of the fed plants over the unfed was even more clearly shown by comparing their seeds, the average weights per seed being as 157 to 100, their total calculated number as 240 to 100, and their total weight as 380 to 100."

"The fed plants, though at the commencement of the experiment in a slight minority, were at the end of the season 20 per cent more numerous than the unfed. In the following spring the young plants which arose on the fed side exceeded those on the unfed side by 18 per cent in number and by 150 per cent in total weight, so that, in spite of the relatively enormous quantity of flower-stalk produced by the fed plants during the previous summer, they had still been able to lay up a far greater store of reserve material."

Similar results were independently reached by Rees, Kellermann, and Von Räumer, who used aphides as food for the plants.

It is noteworthy that the beneficial effect of insect diet, although distinct in the vegetative system, is much more remarkable in relation to reproduction—a fact which explains the unfavourable opinion of other observers.

Other Insectivorous Plants.—Besides the apparently indubitable insect-eaters which we have described, there are some in regard to which fuller information is still desirable. Thus not only Dischidia, an Asiatic genus of Asclepiads, whose pitchers contain internal roots, Martynia, one of the Pedalineæ, but *Caltha dionæfolia*, a species of the same genus as our marsh-marigold, and several Aroids have been called insectivorous. Some South American liverworts (*e.g. Anomoclada mucosa* and *Physiotium cochleariforme*) and a fern (*Elaphoglossum glutinosum*) have been described by Spruce as capturing numerous insects. The basally-united leaves of the common teasel (*Dipsacus*) frequently enclose moats of water in which insects are drowned, and Francis Darwin described protoplasmic filaments apparently emitted by the cells of certain glands within these cups, and which he supposed to absorb the products of decomposition. A similar process has been described by Ludwig as occurring in *Silphium*, a genus allied to the teasel.

Zopf has recently described an interesting fungus (*Arthrobotrya oligospora*), which catches small threadworms in great numbers in its nooses, riddles their bodies with a growth of fine threads (hyphæ), and absorbs the tissues.

Legends. — The existence of insectivorous plants was not recognised in days when fancy, ever nimbler than knowledge, was allowed to trespass unrebuked in the domain of science; yet for that very reason our subject, which affords so many convenient types, shows also how nature-legends arise as of old, by the growing exaggeration and distortion of some real image, as it is reflected from mind to mind. Thus in a well-named medium, the *Review of Reviews*, quoting from "Lucifer" (but it appears not verifiably even there), we recently find this traveller's tale and modern myth: "Mr. Dunstan, naturalist, who has recently returned from Central America, relates the finding of a singular growth in one of the swamps which surround the great lakes of Nicaragua. He was engaged in hunting for specimens when he heard his dog cry out, as if in agony, from a distance. Running to the spot he found him enveloped in a perfect network of what seemed to be fine rope-like tissue of roots and fibres. The plant or vine seemed composed entirely of bare interlacing stems, resembling more than anything else the branches of the weeping willow denuded of its foliage, but of a dark, nearly black hue, and covered with a thick viscid gum which exuded from the pores." Hardly were "the fleshy muscular fibres" severed; "the dog's body was blood-stained, while the skin seemed to have been actually sucked or puckered in spots;" the "twigs curled like living sinuous fingers about Mr. Dunstan's hand"; "its grasp can only be torn away with loss of skin and even of flesh;" "as near as Mr. Dunstan could ascertain its power of suction is contained in a number of infinitesimal mouths or little suckers, which, ordinarily closed, open for the reception of food." "If the substance be animal, the blood is drawn off, and the carcase or refuse then dropped." "A lump of raw meat being thrown to it, in the short space of five minutes the blood will be thoroughly drunk off, and the mass thrown aside." "Its voracity is almost beyond belief." Just as in this story we find a magnified and distorted image of the actual sundew, so in the same way the sober and scientific natural history treatise of Aristotle gradually, though alternately unthinking and fanciful copying, became all but unrecognisably transformed into that marvellous compendium of fabulous natural history, the *Physiologus*, whence herald or gargoyle-carver drew his fantastic images. In earlier beginnings we may perhaps detect the same process at work upon more of Darwin's volumes than the one we have been discussing.

Difficulties.—When Darwin published his book on *Insectivorous Plants*, there were many who disbelieved on the ground that "only animals have the power of digestion." But Morren and others more definitely soon showed the mistakenness of this opinion, for indeed all plants have digestive ferments, and many have two or three. The peculiarity of the insectivorous plant lies then in the outpouring of the digestive juice, not in the possession of it. For even the absorption of organic material is not unique; it is exhibited by the fungi which live among rottenness and by some parasites like the dodder.

How could this exudation of digestive juice begin? May we begin from glands such as those of some Saxifrages, Primulas, Geraniums, and suppose with Darwin that the exudation of digestive fluid began with an exosmose induced by the juices of decaying insects caught among the hairs, and that the habit once set up would be perfected by natural selection? Or may we suppose that the glands and their exuded secretion have always had and still have some meaning, apart altogether from insects; that they express some more direct physiological peculiarity of the plant, and that the insect-catching is after all a minor function? Let us return to the pitcher plants.

Further Difficulties and Criticisms. — How far then are we to regard the pitchers with Hooker, Darwin, and so many others, as primarily insectivorous in function, and to account for them as marvels of the perfecting action of natural selection in progressive adaptation to that strange use? Scepticism and even controversy were rife enough fifteen years ago, but gradually these diminished and disappeared, and most botanists (with whom we may apparently reckon the very latest author, Professor Gœbel, although it is to be regretted that the physiological part of his treatise has still to appear) undoubtedly accept this alike as an established doctrine of vegetable physiology and an admirable special case for the Darwinian theory, explaining every detail of elaborate structure and attractive colour in terms of that view. To this persuasion also the writer was wont fully to belong; witness the undoubting orthodoxy of his article on "Insectivorous Plants" in the *Encyclopædia Britannica* (vol. xiii. 1879). Yet, as better acquaintance with the large Edinburgh collection went on year by year, his faith, it must be confessed, gradually — at first almost insensibly — diminished. Experiments on digestion did not come off so well as Dr. Hooker, still less as Rees and Will, would have it; but this one at first put away as temptations to unbelief — indeed, was ashamed to speak of, for were they not more likely due to some defect in experiment or experimentalist, or if not, to some unlucky dyspepsia of these particular pitchers? The old criticisms of the doctrine, too, were often so unphysiological and in evolution so reactionary, it seemed incredible that they could be of any value!

Timid comparison of notes with Mr. Lindsay, the curator

of the Botanic Garden, than whom these plants have never had a more experienced cultivator, led to a mutual confession of diminished certitude. Mr. Lindsay had often been annoyed by the deterioration of specimens of Nepenthes lent to flower shows, until it occurred to him that this might be due to the loss of the fluid in transit. He gave orders that the next plants so treated should have their pitchers refilled to the proper level on arriving at the show, and again on their return; and when this was done he was gratified to find that the plants no longer suffered. Hence then the fluid is of importance to the plant itself; the pitcher seems a reservoir of the water of transpiration. It is hardly necessary here to recall the distillation of dew from plants by night; the gemmed leaf-tips of the lady's mantle should be familiar to every one who has ever taken a morning stroll along a dewy lane, while every grower of hothouse arums and the like is familiar with the dropping which goes on from the leaf-tips. In 1885 Kny and Zimmermann called attention to the very considerable development in the veins of the Nepenthes leaf of cells of that spirally thickened type which is associated with the carriage of water, and speculated as to its importance for the internal water supply of the plant; while Maury in 1887 insisted that the secreting glands of the Cephalotus pitcher were not the special and essential adaptations towards insect capture and digestion, as which they are commonly described, but mere "water-stomata, which play the part of regulators of transpiration, which give off water when there is an excess, and take it up again when there is a deficiency." Again, "the presence of fluid up to a certain level is the sole cause of the uniformity and polish of the epidermis; one should not see in it a surface specialised as detentive for insects." He denies the digestive agency of the fluid, finds indeed drowned insects, but also infusorians, green algæ, and zoospores all alive, and insists that if the liquid were really very digestive, these could not survive its action. He sums up that the physiological use of pitchers is a general one (associated with transpiration), and not an exceptionally specialised digestive one, as so commonly believed, and lays considerable stress on the comparatively frequent recurrence of pitchers, monstrous as well as normal, among unassociated plant-forms as additional presumptive evidence of their relation to some constant rather than exceptional function of plant-life.

Again, M. Treub, the distinguished director of the famous tropical garden of Buitenzorg (Java), has suggested the internal roots of the Dischidia pitcher to be connected with the reabsorption of water rather than of insect-broth. In a book written before Hooker and Darwin had made Nepenthes and its physiological analogues so famous, Grisebach's *Distribution of Plants* (vol. ii.), we find much speculation on Nepenthes, apparently overlooked by subsequent writers, from which a couple of sentences may be profitably extracted: "So considerable a loss of water should accelerate the circulation of sap much more strongly than would mere transpiration from the surfaces of the leaves. . . . All that the geographical distribution of Nepenthes (Madagascar to New Caledonia) suggests as to their organisation amounts to this, that they inhabit insular climates, of which the atmosphere, abundantly laden with water-vapour, impedes evaporation."

A still more serious criticism is furnished by the latest experiments on the digestion of pitchers and sundews — those of Professor Dubois of Lyons, who has not only the advantage of being apparently the only trained animal physiologist who has yet worked at the question, but also of having at his command the experience and the resources of that vast development of bacteriological science which has grown up, one may practically say entirely, since Hooker and Darwin, Tait, and others carried out the experiments upon which current ideas became established. Without denying then the existence of traces of digestive ferment, such as may be prepared from all or almost all living protoplasm, be it of a seed, a fungus, or a morsel of muscle, he affirms that when the fluid of a pitcher is sterilised so as to exclude the action of bacteria, no digestion takes place—in short, for him such digestion and dissolution of the bodies of insects or artificially supplied food material is simply the work of bacteria, and so comes into line not with digestion, but with putrefaction and decay. He even extends this to fly-traps and sundews.

Need of Further Investigation; Possible Compromise.—It may seem at first sight as if we were but returning to the position of the ancients, yet from either side of the dispute it is easy to correct that impression. Even if our Darwinism be vain, a new explanation has come in sight—that associated with transpiration—and has to be applied in turn. For if pitchers be reservoirs, how do they operate? How shall we explain the glutinous and deliquescent "azerin"—say, as impeding evaporation, or even itself at times helping to draw water from the atmosphere, as the aerial roots do for an orchid? Or does it act, say on sundews, by aiding the transpiratory current, so necessary to the ordinary processes of vegetative life and growth by compelling an exosmose of water to dilute it? Here, then, a new and as yet practically untried field of experiment opens out before us. In fact, despite Darwin's volume, the whole subject of transpiration in sundews and other insectivorous plants, notably of course *Nepenthes*, has still to be experimentally investigated by the vegetable physiologist, before the function of pitchers or tenacles can be really understood. Yet our Darwinian interpretations will not be so easily dismissed, for the movements, the increased and changed secretion of Drosera, still more of Dionæa, are obviously not by mere transpiration to be explained away. And even if the stress hitherto laid upon digestion be more or less given up, and bacteria be admitted as essential factors in the process, must not, even on the new hypothesis, that of regulation of transpiration, the absorption of the soluble products of decay, be all the greater and the more regular, and the importance of insect-catching as a source of nitrogen to the plant be reaffirmed in an altered but even developed form?

Here, indeed, to the writer's mind, we are nearing the probable solution of the case in a compromise, which may indeed give up insectivorism as the main function, yet reinstate it as a secondary one. In all the preceding descriptions of different scenes of the organic drama we have been noting, around what was at first described as the main action, more or less of secondary incident. And now if this apparently main action turn out to be itself but secondary and incidental to a deeper lying and more general action, we may be indeed for a moment confused and perplexed, but our whole interpretation settles itself anew into a richer and more complex form, to which all the preceding interpretations have contributed. Nor is even this new view in turn necessarily final, yet the student-spectator has not lost his pains who can feel and say that while nature's art is long, his time short, experiment fleeting, judgment difficult, yet

> In Nature's infinite book of secrecy
> I can a little read.

CHAPTER IV

MOVEMENT AND NERVOUS ACTION IN PLANTS

Climbing Plants — Darwin's Observations, with Summary — Interpretation of Movements — Movements of Seedlings — Methods of Observation — Theory of Circumnutation.

WE have seen that the sundews and fly-traps have a power of movement as energetic as that of many animals, and a sensitiveness to external stimuli which in its acuteness is not surpassed by that of our own nerves. In our study we closely followed the work of Darwin, for his researches, though by no means infallible, are fundamental, and moreover profoundly suggestive of that living conception of nature which was so characteristic of his work. In order to gain more complete possession of his point of view — which is indeed that of Modern Botany — let us still, as it were, continue to walk in his garden and look at plants through his eyes. With this purpose we shall first take a rapid survey of Darwin's observations on Climbing Plants as they are set forth in one of his volumes.[1]

Climbing Plants. — Among many different orders of plants, and in all parts of the world, there are climbers which reach the air and the light on the shoulders of their stronger fellows. They insinuate themselves among the

[1] *The Movements and Habits of Climbing Plants* (London, 1875).

straggling branches of their neighbours, or twine themselves around the upright stems, or moor themselves by sensitive elastic tendrils to the twigs of their bearers; thus reaching out of the crowded life of the ground herbage, or out of the darkness and closeness of the jungle, to room and fresh air and sunlight above.

Darwin arranged these climbers in four grades. Rising a little above the crowd of those which merely scramble over surrounding bushes, there are the hook-climbers, such as Jack-run-the-hedge (*Galium Aparine*), and root-climbers, such as the Ivy. More efficient are the twiners, like the hop (*Humulus*) and the Honeysuckle (*Lonicera*), but the climbing habit is most frequently and most perfectly exhibited by plants with sensitive prehensile organs, either leaves or tendrils.

Let us consider these different kinds of climbers more precisely, recognising, however, that the classification is merely one of general convenience, for there are gradations between scramblers and hook-climbers, between creeping plants and root-climbers, between those which climb by their leaves and the tendril-bearers.

The hook-climbers are least effective, being little more than scramblers well equipped with hooks which are caught up in the surrounding vegetation. Thus many brambles and roses are merely scramblers, while the New Zealand *Rubus squarrosus* and a rose known as *Rosa setigera* may be fairly called climbers. The habit is very well illustrated by those oriental plants which are often called Rotangs (*e.g. Calamus extensus*), which with barbed branches insinuate themselves and grow up through their more vigorous neighbours. A more familiar example is the Jack-run-the-hedge, whose stem and leaves are beset with backward-directed hooks most efficient in binding the plant to the growth of the hedgerow.

Creeping plants, such as Ground-ivy (*Nepeta Glechoma*) and Strawberry, spread along the ground or up the woodside bank, sending out long shoots which are at intervals rooted in the soil. These suggest the next set of climbing plants — the root-climbers, such as the common Ivy. These ascend slowly, fixing themselves by rootlets which grow away from the light and become glued to the stems of trees or to the surfaces of rocks. We all know the little brown roots by means of which the ivy clings so closely that if you pull a piece off by force the roots often break at their origin from the stem and not from their attachment. There are many other root-climbers, such as *Tecoma radicans* common in the Southern States, some species of Bignonia, and many Figs (*Ficus repens*, etc.). The beautiful night-flowering Cactus (*Cereus nyctiflora*), often called "queen of the night," also affords a not uncommon transition to these true climbers; scrambling as it does over rocks, and freely giving off at almost any portion of its surface adventitious roots which soon fix the plant, but no doubt also have a genuinely absorbent function as well.

The twiners, such as the Hop and the Honeysuckle, differ from those already mentioned, for as they grow their stems have a marked power of movement, bending and bowing to all sides, and thus encircling their support. Most twine in a definite direction; thus the hop twines in a right-handed spiral (*i.e.* with the sun, or with the hands of a watch lying face upwards), while the majority resemble the French Bean (*Phaseolus multiflorus*) in winding to the left. The Bitter-sweet (*Solanum Dulcamara*, seems to twine indifferently in either direction, and the stem of the Chili-nettle (*Loasa*) may change its direction in the course of its climbing.

The next two sets of climbing plants are closely united.

The leaf-climbers have clasping petioles as in Clematis and Tropæolum, or hook themselves up by the tips of their leaves as in Gloriosa; most of them also revolve like the twiners, and in this way bring their leaves into contact with adjacent branches. When they are young the leaf-stalk or the leaf-tip, or even the whole surface of the leaf (in the climbing fumitory, *Corydalis claviculata*), is sensitive to contact, bends towards the side on which pressure is exerted, and thus clasps the plant to its support.

The tendril-bearers, such as the pea and the vine and the passion-flower, are the most evolved climbers, for they have prehensile organs specially adapted for this function. These prehensile organs or tendrils may be modified leaflets as in the pea, or modified leaves as in *Lathyrus Aphaca*, or flower-stalks as in the vine, or even branches in some rare cases. The shoots of the tendril-bearers revolve as those of the leaf-climbers do, and the tendrils themselves move round and round. Thus the tendrils are brought into contact with surrounding objects, to the touch of which they are often finely sensitive. They curve to what they touch and link themselves around it, after which they usually grow stronger and thicker, and by coiling into a spiral raise the plant nearer to its support.

Darwin's Observations on Climbing and Twining Plants. — Having now classified the climbing plants as Darwin did, we shall inquire more carefully into what he has told us of their life.

In regard to twining plants let us quote one of Darwin's observations: "When the shoot of a hop rises from the ground, the two or three first-formed joints or internodes are straight and remain stationary; but the next formed, whilst very young, may be seen to bend to one side and to travel slowly round towards all points of the compass, moving, like the hands of a watch, with the sun. The movement very soon acquires its full ordinary velocity. From seven observations made during August on shoots proceeding from a plant which had been cut down, and on another plant during April, the average rate during hot weather and during the day is 2 hours 8 minutes for each revolution; and none of the revolutions varied much from this rate. The revolving movement continues as long as the plant continues to grow; but each separate internode, as it becomes old, ceases to move."

The characteristic movement is a turning to all sides in succession. In so doing the stem usually becomes twisted upon itself, and perhaps thus gains in strength, as a rope becomes firmer as it is more twisted. The revolutions continue, though not with equal rapidity, during the night as well as during the day; the orbit described by the tip of the shoot becomes wider and wider as the shoots grow longer, and the chance of meeting with some upright support becomes greater and greater. The shoot is arrested at length by contact with a support, but the free part goes on revolving. "As this continues, higher and higher points are brought into contact with the support and are arrested; and so onwards to the extremity; and thus the shoot winds round its support."

There is a general uniformity in the behaviour of twining plants, but the direction and rate of revolution vary in different kinds. Thus, as we have mentioned, the majority revolve in a direction opposite to that of the hands of a watch, but many follow the sun; one shoot may make its revolution in little more than an hour, while another may take a whole day. But at present we are chiefly concerned with the general fact that these twiners do move round and round.

Leaf-climbers are in their behaviour in some respects intermediate between twiners and tendril-bearers. Like twining plants they show a revolution of young shoots, but with a marked tendency to change the direction of circuit; they approach the tendril-bearers in having petioles or leaf-tips sensitive to contact and able to clasp their support. This sensitiveness is often exquisitely fine, indeed it seems more delicate than the tactile sense of most animals. Thus Darwin observed a petiole responding to the excessively slight but continued pressure of a loop of soft thread weighing only $\frac{1}{16}$ of a grain. The response is a bending towards the side which is touched, and sometimes begins a few minutes after contact. After clasping has been effected the leaf-stalks become stronger and more woody, often acquiring a stem-like internal structure. It is interesting to observe that while most species of Clematis and Tropæolum are effective leaf-climbers, there are some species of more sluggish constitution, in which both the mobility and the sensitiveness of the petiole are enfeebled, or even lost altogether.

Both mobility and sensitiveness reach their climax in the tendril-bearers. In the common pea the tendrils revolve in ellipses, taking about an hour and a half to complete their orbit. "Whilst young and about an inch in length, with the leaflets on the petiole only partially expanded, they are highly sensitive; a single light touch with a twig on the inferior or concave surface near the tip caused them to bend quickly, as did occasionally a loop of thread weighing $\frac{1}{2}$ of a grain." The long and thick tendrils of the vine — modified flower-stalks in structure — are much less active, but move from side to side, or in narrow elliptical revolutions. In both the pea and the vine, and in most tendril-bearers, the tendrils contract spirally a day or two after they have clasped some object In this way they become apparently shorter and obviously more elastic, not only drawing the shoot nearer its support, but forming cables which do not easily snap. "I have," Darwin says, "more than once gone on purpose during a gale to watch a Bryony growing in an exposed hedge, with its tendrils attached to the surrounding bushes; and as the thick and thin branches were tossed to and fro by the wind, the tendrils, had they not been excessively elastic, would instantly have been torn off and the plant thrown prostrate. But as it was, the Bryony safely rode out the gale, like a ship with two anchors down, and with a long range of cable ahead to serve as a spring as she surges to the storm."

As to the more precise nature of the movement, it is enough in the meantime to notice that the whole tendril — excepting the base and the tip — is continuously curved, bending in succession to each point of the compass. On a thick tendril a line of paint may be drawn; this line, if drawn on the surface which chanced to be convex at the time, would first become lateral, then concave, then lateral, and finally convex as at first.

But we should also give some illustration of the great sensitiveness of tendrils. To those of the passion-flower (*Passiflora gracilis*) Darwin gave the highest place. "A bit of platinum wire $\frac{1}{50}$ of a grain in weight, gently placed on the concave point, caused a tendril to become hooked, as did a loop of soft, thin, cotton thread $\frac{1}{32}$ of a grain. With the tendrils of several other plants, loops weighing $\frac{1}{16}$ of a grain sufficed. The point of a tendril of *Passiflora gracilis* began to move distinctly in 25 seconds after a touch, and in many cases after 30 seconds."

Summary. — To sum up after Darwin: the first action of a tendril is to place itself in a proper position; if a twining plant or a tendril gets by any accident into an inclined position, it soon bends upwards, though secluded from the light, the guiding stimulus being the attraction of gravity; climbing plants bend towards the light by a movement closely analogous to the incurvation which causes them to revolve; the spontaneous revolving movement is independent of any outward stimulus, but is contingent on the youth of the part and on vigorous health, which again depends on a proper temperature and other favourable conditions of life; tendrils, and the petioles or tips of the leaves of leaf-climbers, and apparently certain roots, all have the power of movement when touched, and bend quickly towards the touched side; tendrils contract spirally soon after clasping a support, but not after a mere temporary curvature (due to pressure which is not permanent), and they ultimately contract spirally if they have not come into contact with any object.

Interpretation of Movements. — But the student naturally asks what interpretation Darwin put upon these movements of climbing plants. It will be easier to answer this after we have considered what he thought of the many other movements which plants exhibit. Meantime, however, a partial answer may be given.

In the first place, it is plain that the climbing habit is a useful one, such as would tend to persist in nature. "The advantage gained by climbing is to reach the light and free air with as little expenditure of organic matter as possible."

In the second place, the habit of climbing is not an occasional freak; it is of widespread occurrence among plants. Of the fifty-nine alliances into which Lindley divided flowering plants, thirty-five, according to Darwin, include twiners, leaf-climbers, or tendril-bearers. Moreover, the most different organs — stems, branches, flower-stalks, petioles, midribs of the leaf and leaflets, and apparently aerial roots — all possess this power. Not unnaturally, therefore, did Darwin regard the powers of climbers as inherent in all the higher plants. In crowded surroundings, where it is of advantage to rise, some plants have retained and developed the powers of moving and feeling which are latent in all.

In the third place, while the powers of climbers are often markedly influenced by temperature, by light, by gravity, and other factors in their environment, it is certain that these do not explain the movement, except, of course, in so far as the health of the plant depends ultimately upon the sufficiency of its surroundings. In short, the movements are manifestations of the internal life of the plant.

But by what means within the plant are they produced? Of this in his volume on Climbing Plants Darwin says little, nor can we even now say anything very complete. This is not greatly to be wondered at, for as we have little minute knowledge as to the processes of contraction in animals where we know that these are located in definite structures — the muscles — it is not surprising that we know still less as to the movements of plants which have no specialised contractile elements that we can recognise.

Sachs, Dr. de Vries, and others have suggested that the rotating movement — say of a twining shoot — is due to unequal growth now on one side and now on another, and that this again depends on altered water-tension or turgescence in the growing cells. This suggestion was accepted by Darwin, although he did not believe that it could apply to those cases where rapid movement follows a slight touch. This is obviously a difficulty. Furthermore, the suggestion that unequal growth on different sides of the stem explains the revolving movements has to face the fact that the rotating movement may continue without there being any observable growth.

Without denying that the altered water-tension and unequal growth explain some of the facts, it seems to others more convenient to take refuge in the hypothesis that there are in longitudinal rows along the moving shoot certain cells which retain the power of contracting and expanding — of passing rapidly from one state of water-tension to another — and that these determine the movement of the whole shoot.

For our present purpose what is especially important is that we appreciate the plant world as living; instead, therefore, of here prolonging our discussion of the theories held in regard to the movements of climbers, let us return to the general standpoint of Darwin's volume, of which the last paragraph may be quoted:—

"It has often been vaguely asserted that plants are distinguished from animals by not having the power of movement. It should rather be said that plants acquire and display this power only when it is of some advantage to them; this being of comparatively rare occurrence, as they are affixed to the ground, and food is brought to them by the air and rain. We see how high in the scale of organisation a plant may rise when we look at one of the more perfect tendril-bearers. It first places the tendrils ready for action, as a polypus places its tentacula. If the tendril be displaced, it is acted on by the force of gravity and rights itself. It is acted on by the light, and bends towards or from it, or disregards it, whichever may be most advantageous. During several days the tendrils or internodes, or both, spontaneously revolve with a steady motion. The tendril strikes some object, and quickly curls round and firmly grasps it. In the course of some hours it contracts into a spire, dragging up the stem, and forming an excellent spring. All movements now cease. By growth the tissues soon become wonderfully strong and durable. The tendril has done its work, and has done it in an admirable manner."

Movements of Seedlings.—We have seen how Darwin began to believe that all plants in some degree possessed the powers of movement which are conspicuously developed in the climbers. To test this opinion he and his son Francis began to watch and experiment with many kinds of plants, and the results of their study are told in the sequel to the work on Climbing Plants, a volume entitled *The Power of Movement in Plants* (London, 1880). As before, let us follow Darwin, and first of all in watching the life of a seedling.

The seed lies on the damp ground, covered perhaps with leaves which have fallen from the trees. As water finds its way into the seed, as the life within begins to gather strength, the young root or radicle makes its appearance. It begins at once to move round and round. But its movements are influenced by gravity, and it bends downwards, following a more or less spiral course towards the ground. Darwin believed that "sensitiveness to gravitation resides in the tip, which transmits some influence to the adjoining parts, causing them to bend." When the tip of the root reaches the soil it bores into it, aided by the continued movement of the radicle, and this boring is easier if some soil has fallen upon the seed and fixed it, or if fine root-hairs from the top of the radicle have moored the seed to the surface. Then as the radicle grows longer its tip is forced into the soil.

There it can no longer bend round and round, but it may try to do so. And sometimes the tip will reach a crevice, or it may be an earthworm's burrow, in which it can move more freely. "When a tip encounters a stone or other obstacle in the ground, or even earth more compact on one side than the other, the root will bend away as much as it can from the obstacle or the more resisting earth, and will thus follow with unerring skill a line of least resistance."

The tip of the radicle is a very sensitive structure: "it was excited by an attached bead of shellac weighing less than $\frac{1}{200}$ of a grain;" it bends towards moisture and away from light: it always responds to the attraction of earth even when grown in entirely abnormal conditions. "If the tip be lightly pressed or burnt or cut, it transmits an influence to the upper adjoining part, causing it to bend away from the affected side; and, what is more surprising, the tip can distinguish between a slightly harder and softer object, by which it is simultaneously pressed on opposite sides." "It is hardly an exaggeration," Darwin concluded, "to say that the tip of the radicle thus endowed, and having the power of directing the movements of the adjoining parts, acts like the brain of one of the lower animals."

But the movements of seedlings are not confined to the radicle. From the seed there also emerges the young stem or plumule, almost always bent in the form of an arch, the tender tip remaining within the protecting seed-coats until the first obstacles to growth have been overcome. If the seed be buried the arch breaks through the ground, and is helped in doing this by slight movements. The young stem grows blindly but unerringly upwards towards light and air, as the root downwards towards moisture and darkness; we cannot yet give any full or sufficient mechanical explanation why, though it is here only too easy to cloak our ignorance under learned nomenclature.[1]

As the arch grows upwards, freeing itself from the soil, the seed-leaves or cotyledons, if not already in use as store-

---

[1] It does not seem necessary to encumber this narrative or the student's mind at this stage with the numerous technical terms applied to movements in relation to gravitation, light, moisture, etc., since these are only too apt to correspond to no definite mental images of any kind, but be used as mere illusory explanations in terms of "inherent properties." See next chapter.

houses of food, will be raised above the ground and expanded in the air. Sooner or later the arch straightens into an upright shoot. Both in the young shoot and in the expanded cotyledons there is power of movement; they are exquisitely sensitive to light and to gravitation.

The power of movement does not cease when the shoot becomes a stem with leaves and branches. "If we look, for instance, at a great Acacia tree, we may feel assured that every one of the innumerable growing shoots is constantly describing small ellipses; as is each petiole, sub-petiole, and leaflet. The latter, as well as ordinary leaves, generally move up and down in nearly the same vertical plane, so that they describe very narrow ellipses. The flower-peduncles are likewise continually circumnutating. If we could look beneath the ground, and our eyes had the power of a microscope, we should see the tip of each rootlet endeavouring to sweep small ellipses or circles, as far as the pressure of the surrounding earth permitted. All this astonishing amount of movement has been going on year after year since the time when, as a seedling, the tree first emerged from the ground."

Methods of Observation. — But how can these movements be seen and measured? In some of the more marked cases, as of twiners and climbers, there is no difficulty whatever. We need only observe the position of the plant at intervals of hours and days. Or if we note the position of a growing shoot in the garden as it bends over to one side, and fix a piece of string, by means of a couple of stakes, so that it lies in a line with the shoot when looked at from above, we can, if we return in half an hour or so, plainly see that the shoot has moved through a large angle.

But there are of course more delicate modes of observation. Darwin gives many figures representing, *e.g.* the path of the young stem of a seedling cabbage during ten hours. How did Darwin get this record?

"Plants growing in pots were protected wholly from the light, or had light admitted from above, or on one side, as the case might require, and were covered above by a large horizontal sheet of glass, and with another vertical sheet on one side. A glass filament, not thicker than a horsehair, and from a quarter to three-quarters of an inch in length, was affixed to the part to be observed by means of shellac dissolved in alcohol. The solution was allowed to evaporate, until it became so thick that it set hard in two or three seconds, and "it never injured the tissues, even the tips of tender radicles, to which it was applied." (?) To the end of the glass filament an excessively minute bead of black sealing-wax was cemented, below or behind which a bit of card with a black dot was fixed to a stick driven into the ground. The weight of the filament was so slight that even small leaves were not perceptibly pressed down. The bead and the dot on the card were viewed through the horizontal or vertical glass-plate, (according to the position of the object), and when one exactly covered the other, a dot was made on the glass-plate with a sharply-pointed stick dipped in thick Indian ink. Other dots were made at short intervals of time, and these were afterwards joined by straight lines."

Of course the result was not a picture, only a record of the plant's path, showing nothing more than the general character of the movement.

Another method, which, however, is only in a few cases practicable, is to allow the moving parts — radicles, for instance — to trace their own paths, to write, as it were, their own diary, on smoked plates of glass. Figures of these root-tracks are given by Darwin in abundance, and the student, in this case as the preceding, may profitably endeavour to make them for himself.

Darwin's Theory of Modified Circumnutation. — Darwin's observations led him to conclude that every growing part of every plant is continually moving, though often on a small scale. And as the most prevalent form of movement is like that of a climbing plant, which bends successively to all points of the compass, so that the tip revolves, Darwin applied to it the term circumnutation. This term he explains as follows: "If we observe a circumnutating stem, which happens at the time to be bent, we will say towards the north, it will be found gradually to bend more and more easterly until it faces the east; and so onwards to the south, then to the west, and back again to the north. If the movement had been quite regular the apex would have described a circle, or rather, as the stem is always growing upwards, a circular spiral. But it generally describes irregular elliptical or oval figures; for the apex, after pointing in any one direction, commonly moves back to the opposite side, not, however, returning along the same line."

In this "universally present movement" Darwin found "the basis of groundwork for the acquirement, according to the requirements of the plant, of the most diversified movements." His particular thesis was that the great sweeps made by the twiners and by tendrils, the movements of leaves when they go to sleep at night, the movements of various organs to the light or away from it, and even the movement of stems towards the zenith and of roots towards the centre of the earth, are all modified forms of circumnutation, which is omnipresent while growth lasts. In regard to the two last sets of movement he believed, of course, in the influence of light and gravitation, but he regarded these as simply operating upon spontaneous processes of circumnutation, hastening, diminishing, or otherwise modifying them. While maintaining this theory of circumnutation Darwin acknowledged that it did not explain all movements; he did not propose to apply it to the collapse of the Sensitive plant's leaves when they are touched, or to the movement of the stimulated Sundew and Venus Fly-Trap, or to the movement of the Barberry's stamens when they are jostled by an insect's legs.

In regard to the means by which the circumnutating movements are brought about, Darwin expressed himself in his *Movements of Plants* more definitely than he had done in the previous volume. Following several German botanists, he emphasised the importance of the turgescence or state of water-tension of the cells of the plant, and he also recognised the extensibility of the cell-walls. "On the whole," he says, "we may at present conclude that increased growth, first on one side and then on another, is a secondary effect, and that the increased turgescence of the cells, together with the extensibility of their walls, is the primary cause of the movement of circumnutation."

Having stated the general thesis of Darwin's book, namely, that most of the movements of plants are modified forms of circumnutation, and his general conception of the internal processes involved, we may next briefly discuss the movements of plants in their relation to gravitation, light, and other external influences. In so doing we shall not insist upon Darwin's generalisation, for perhaps no part of his work has met with more adverse criticism, as notably on the part of Sachs, than this. It is indeed the opinion of most botanists that Darwin's theory of circumnutation was overstrained.

CHAPTER V

MOVEMENTS OF PLANTS — *continued*

Movements in relation to Gravitation — Light-seeking and Light-avoiding Movements — Rationale of Light-seeking and Light-avoiding Movements — The Sleep of Plants — Mr. Francis Darwin's recent Discussion of Plant Movements — Summary and Conclusion.

Movements of Plants in Relation to Gravitation. — We are so familiar with the fact that stems grow upwards and roots downwards that we perhaps do not think of it as in the least remarkable that one part of a plant should persistently grow against and the other part in the direction of the acting force of gravity. Of course the student may be tempted to ask what roots would do up in the air or what stems would do down in the ground, or how they could grow otherwise than up and down, but these questions are not exactly to the point — which is this, that even when young plants are taken from their natural conditions, when they are turned upside down or grown on a rapidly rotating wheel, still the opposite tendencies of root and stem assert themselves.

Let us see how the behaviour of roots and stems to the force of gravity is experimentally demonstrated.

If seeds of peas and beans which have germinated in

loose soil, and have little straight radicles, be carefully removed, and suspended in the air under a damp bell-jar with the radicles pointing upwards or horizontally, in the course of a few hours the radicles will all have turned downwards.

In the same way the growing shoots of plants may be placed or artificially forced to grow in a horizontal position, but if the shoot be strong enough and be not, for instance, naturally a creeper, its character asserts itself as soon as it is free from restraint, and the stem grows upwards.

As long ago as 1806 Knight tried the effect of growing young plants on a rotating wheel. When an apparatus of this sort is devised, with seedlings suitably fixed on a rotating disc, the young roots always grow outwards and the young stems inwards. When the plane of rotation is vertical the direct influence of gravitation is counteracted, its direction being continually altered; but in relation to the so-called "centrifugal force" the roots and the stems grow in consistently antagonistic directions, the stems against, the roots in the direction of the acting force.

There is a more modern apparatus called a klinostat, a clockwork arrangement by which germinating seeds are slowly rotated in a vertical plane, and as the relation of the parts to the earth's axis is constantly changing, the direct action of gravity is counteracted; the result being, as we would expect, that the young roots and stems grow in totally indefinite fashion.

No one will suppose that in normal conditions the roots simply sink downwards passively, for they will force their way into quicksilver, and besides the stem is influenced in an exactly opposite way. It is certain that the parts of plants are influenced by gravity, but not passively; they are living organs.

It seems likely that the roots and the stems, differing as

they do in structure, have the water-tension of their cells, and secondarily, their growth differently affected by the force of gravity; but other explanations are in the field. Some botanists go so far as to suppose a distinct stem-protoplasm and a distinct root-protoplasm reacting in opposite ways to given stimuli. Hence we see that after all the research and discussion which has taken place the subject is still far from being cleared up. Here, as in the allied or, at any rate, intermingled problem of explaining the mechanism of light-seeking and light-avoiding, the student must guard against the too common habit of finding an explanation in what is but a technical nomenclature, and not cease to ask himself the child's puzzling questions of why does this stem grow up and that root grow down merely because he is told to call them in longer words "negatively" or "positively geotropic." For though we may all laugh with Molière at old-world medicine, it is no easy matter to leave its *virtus dormitiva* out of our minds.

Darwin laid emphasis on the very tip of the radicle. "In the case of the radicles of several, probably of all seedling plants, sensitiveness to gravitation is confined to the tip, which transmits an influence to the adjoining upper part, causing it to bend towards the centre of the earth." When the tips were amputated the power was lost until a new tip was formed. Subsequent experiments do not, however, confirm this opinion, if indeed they have not disproved it.

Darwin also made a large number of experiments showing how a radicle on whose tip some minute object was fastened, or some slight injury inflicted, bent towards the free or uninjured side. But when the stimulus is applied not to the side of the tip, but to the growing region a little above the tip, the bending takes place towards the stimulus.

In regard to such experiments, however, critics have justly pointed out that we must be exceedingly careful, with plants as well as with animals, in drawing conclusions as to normal life from facts observed when injuries are inflicted, however apparently slight these injuries may be; and this experiment must therefore be given up.

Besides being affected by gravity and by light, roots are very sensitive to moisture. They always grow towards the greater moisture, sometimes even against gravity. Thus if seeds be allowed to germinate in a sieve filled with damp sawdust, the roots first grow downwards as usual, but after they have descended through the sieve into the dry air, the direction of their growth changes, and they grow up again into the moisture.

Light - seeking and Light - avoiding Movements. — Every one must have noticed that plants which have grown in the recess of a narrow window are often very markedly curved towards the light. The same light-seeking can be readily shown by experiment, for if seedlings are grown in a box which is illumined by a single aperture they all turn their young stems towards the path of the light. Some sedentary animals, such as the Serpula worms, which make for themselves twisted tubes of lime, have the same habit of bending to the light.

Some of Darwin's observations show the extreme sensitiveness of certain seedlings to light. "The cotyledons of Phalaris became curved towards a distant lamp, which emitted so little light that a pencil held vertically close to the plants did not cast any shadow which the eye could perceive on a white card. These cotyledons, therefore, were affected by a difference in the amount of light on their two sides, which the eye could not distinguish." Darwin also noticed that if seedlings kept in a dark place were laterally illuminated by a small wax taper for only two or three minutes at intervals of about three-quarters of an hour, they all became bowed to the point where the taper had been held. This convinced him that the excitement from the light was due not so much to its actual amount as to the difference in amount between that previously received. "Light seems to act on the tissues of plants almost in the same manner as it does on the nervous system of animals."

Usually the movement is towards the light, especially in the case of stems, but this is not invariably the case. Thus the shoots of the ivy bend away from, not towards the light, and so do the tendrils of the vine, of the Virginian creeper (*Ampelopsis hederacea*), and some other plants. We can easily understand that it is advantageous for tendrils to seek shaded recesses, for in so doing they will usually come nearer the support to which they cling, although of course this advantage must not blind us to the necessity of a physiological explanation.

As most roots seek the ground their reactions to light are not readily tested, except in artificial conditions. But by means of the klinostat — the rotating apparatus which we have already mentioned — it is possible to grow seedlings illumined in one direction only, and with the influence of gravitation eliminated. Then it is seen that some roots bend towards and others away from the light. Of roots which in natural conditions always bend away from the light, the climbing roots of the ivy are the most familiar examples. Or the following simple experiment may be made, following the directions of Professor Detmer's laboratory manual of practical vegetable physiology — a work which will be of great use to the student (and which can also be obtained in translation): A glass filled with water is closed with a lid of fine muslin; on the top of this are placed germinating seeds of white mustard (*Sinapis alba*); the whole is covered with a bell-jar and placed in the dark. The young stem grows straight up, the young root grows straight down into the water. Then light is allowed to fall upon the plant, in one direction only, through a narrow slit. In a few hours the young stem has curved towards, the young root away from the light.

Darwin's experiments led him to conclude that the sensitiveness to light was localised in the tips, *e.g.* of the cotyledons of Phalaris and Avena, of the young stems of Brassica and Beta, and of the radicles of Sinapis. There seemed to be a transmission of influence from the tip to the other parts, causing them to bend. "It is an interesting experiment to place caps over the tips of the cotyledons of Phalaris, and to allow a very little light to enter through minute orifices on one side of the caps, for the lower part of the cotyledons will then bend to this side, and not to the side which has been brightly illuminated during the whole time."

The commonest position of leaves and cotyledons during the day is one more or less transverse to the direction of the light, and this also Darwin believed to be due to a modified circumnutation; but few would now agree with him in this interpretation. In some plants in which the leaflets are provided with little swollen cushions or pulvini at their base, they move upwards or downwards or twist laterally when the sun shines very brightly upon them, as in the well-known " compass-plant " (Silphium) ; by directing their edges towards the light they avoid the injurious effects of too intense illumination.

It is easy to understand that it is advantageous for most plants to bend towards the light, for thus their leaves are in a better position to use the power of the sunlight on which the life of the plant so much depends. On the other hand, it is also advantageous that the aerial rootlets of the ivy or the tendrils of the vine should turn away from the light.

But it is difficult for us to form any conception of the reason why different plants or different parts of the same plants should be affected by the light in opposite ways. Thus the flower-stalks of the ivy-leaved toad-flax (*Linaria Cymbalaria*), which so often drapes our old walls with beauty, at first bend towards the light, but turn in the opposite direction after the flowers are fertilised, and the time approaches for planting the seed in a crevice.

As to the causes of the light-seeking or light-avoiding movements, in their usual forms they are possible only as long as the moving parts continue to grow. Now as light usually exerts a retarding influence on growth, the side of the plant which is shaded grows more quickly than the side which is lighted, hence the plant bends towards the light. But this will not explain light-avoiding, and so we are led to recognise, as before, that the effect of the light on the living matter of different parts of the plant or of different plants is not always the same.

Rationale of Light-seeking and Light-avoiding Movements. — But when we inquire more precisely into the influence of the light, a hundred difficulties beset us. How far was Darwin right in supposing that light simply modifies an existing spontaneous movement of circumnutation? How far are others warranted in assuming that there are in different parts of the plant specially contractile cells which are affected in various ways by stimuli? in other words, how far may the movements be independent of growth? Or if the movements be entirely dependent upon growth, how far is this the result of a change in the water-tension or turgescence of the cells exerting pressure on their internal surfaces, as Sachs and De Vries would say; or is Klebs wholly wrong in regarding the turgescence rather as a symptom than as a cause, and in referring growth to unknown properties of the protoplasm?

And even if we accept the general conclusion that the altered growth is due to a modification of turgescence in the growing cells, to what is the change of turgescence due? — to a change in the elasticity of the cell-wall, as Sachs, Pfeffer, Wiesner, and others suggest; or to a change in the osmotic properties of the cell-sap, the stimulus promoting, according to De Vries, the formation of substances which are osmotically active; or to a change in the permeability of the protoplasm, resulting directly from the influence of light, as Vines believes? Finally, according to Wortmann, growth depends on three factors — the osmotic force within the cell, the extensibility of the cell-walls, and the relative abundance of surrounding water. Or if we turn to a recent Botanical Journal, we find Noll maintaining that curvature is due to a greater extensibility of the cell-walls on the convex side and to a diminished extensibility on the concave side — opposite effects produced by the mysterious activity of the parietal protoplasm; and we find Wortmann denying this, saying that the curvature is due to a movement of the protoplasm which in the region of growth alters the thickness and tension of the cell-wells, distributing its materials so that the two sides are unequally thickened.

Thus the student may see that as in regard to structural problems, such as the real nature of the pitchers of pitcher plants, so in regard to physiological problems, such as this of the movement of plants in relation to light and other stimuli, there is much difference of opinion. The reason for this is perfectly obvious — the problem is so complex, so many factors have to be considered. The history of the investigation is, as in all other cases, one of progressive analysis. That plants move towards the light in virtue of "heliotropism" is obviously a truism; that the "heliotropism" may be due to unequal growth expresses the first step in the analysis; the unequal growth is associated with altered water-tension, etc., in the cells expresses another step, and so on. The problem is to discover all the observable conditions of the movement before finally confessing that what remains unexplained is due to some still unknown property or power of the living matter or protoplasm.

This above all the student should recognise that the plant is in all its actions no mere mechanical system, completely explicable according to the facts of mechanics, hydrostatics, and the like, but a living organism. And just as no one will pretend to give a "mechanical explanation" of how a Serpula worm makes its calcareous tube towards the light, nor pretend to be content with calling the animal "heliotropic," so we must avoid both extremes in regard to plants.

The Sleep of Plants.—Every one has noticed how the three leaflets of the clover and the wood-sorrel change their position as the light of day grows and wanes; they are expanded during the day, and fold downwards in the evening. Many may have observed similar movements in Lupine and Melilot, Mimosa and Acacia. Indeed these movements are very common, and were noticed by early naturalists such as Pliny. Since Linnæus wrote his famous essay called *Somnus Plantarum* they have been spoken of as the sleep of plants.

The movements are sometimes very marked, changing the whole appearance of the plants; thus " a bush of *Acacia farnesiana* appears at night as if covered with little dangling bits of string instead of leaves."

Although sleep-movements are very general, their amount and their nature are greatly diversified. Thus Darwin enumerates 37 genera in which the leaves or leaflets rise, and 32 genera in which they sink at night. In some species the leaves sleep, but not the cotyledons;

in a larger number the cotyledons sleep, but not the leaves; in many both sleep, but in widely different positions. Yet if sleep occur the general result is always the same; the blade is placed in such a position at night that its upper surface is exposed as little as possible to full radiation.

The movements are without doubt associated with the daily alternation of light and darkness; but it is the difference in the illumination rather than the darkness which excites the change, for Darwin showed that in several species, if the leaves have not been brightly illuminated during the day, they do not sleep at night. Moreover, in the North, where the sun does not set, Mimosa still goes regularly to sleep; and by artificial light and darkness the daily movements may be reversed. "The presence of light or its absence cannot be supposed to be the direct cause of the movements, for these are wonderfully diversified even with the leaflets of the same leaf, although all have of course been similarly exposed. The movements depend on innate causes, and are of an adaptive nature. The alternations of light and darkness merely give notice to the leaves that the period has arrived for them to move in a certain manner. We may infer from the fact of several plants (Tropæolum, Lupine, etc.) not sleeping unless they have been well illuminated during the day, that it is not the actual decrease of the light in the evening, but the contrast between the amount at this hour and during the early part of the day, which excites the leaves to modify their ordinary mode of circumnutation. As the leaves of most plants assume their proper diurnal position in the morning, although light be excluded, and as the leaves of some plants continue to move in the normal manner in darkness during at least a whole day, we may conclude that the periodicity of their movements is to a certain extent inherited. The strength of such inheritance differs much in different species, and seems never to be very rigid; for plants have been introduced from all parts of the world into our gardens and greenhouses; and if their movements had been at all strictly fixed in relation to the alternations of day and night, they would have slept in this country at very different hours, which is not the case; moreover, it has been observed that sleeping plants in their native homes change their times of sleep with the changing seasons."

The movements Darwin explained in two ways: "firstly, by alternately increased growth on the opposite sides of the leaves, preceded by increased turgescence of the cells; and secondly, by means of a pulvinus or aggregate of small cells, generally destitute of chlorophyll, which becomes alternately more turgescent on nearly opposite sides; and this turgescence is not followed by growth except during the early age of the plant." The movement may be almost the same whether a pulvinus be present or not, but in the former case the course of the leaves is more regularly elliptical, and the movements are continued for a much longer period in the life of the plant.

The position occupied by the leaves at night indicates that the benefit they derive is "the protection of their upper surfaces from radiation into the open sky; and in many cases the mutual protection of all the parts from cold by their being brought into close approximation." In evidence of this Darwin showed that leaves compelled to remain extended horizontally at night, suffered much more from radiation than those which were allowed to assume their normal vertical position.

"Any one who had never observed continuously a sleeping plant, would naturally suppose that the leaves moved only in the evening when going to sleep, and in the morning when awaking; but he would be quite mistaken, for we have found no exception to the rule that leaves which sleep continue to move during the whole twenty-four hours; they move, however, more quickly when going to sleep and when awaking than at other times."

Exceptional Developments of Plant Movement, the Telegraph Plant, Sensitive Plant, etc.—The most remarkable case of continuous movement is that of the Indian Telegraph plant (*Desmodium* or *Hedysarum gyrans*). Its leaves have three leaflets—a large median one, and two lateral ones which are rudimentary. The main part moves a little during the day and has a remarkable sleep movement, but the lateral leaflets which do not sleep move constantly, describing with a series of little jerks minute circles. Each revolution sometimes occupies little over a minute.

The term sleep is often applied, as Linnæus applied it, not only to leaves, but also to the petals of many flowers which close at night. This seems to depend rather upon a difference of temperature determining differences in turgescence than on a difference of illumination, and it has the effect of sheltering the internal parts of the flower from cold winds, rain, and over-radiation. Here certainly Darwin's suggestion of "modified circumnutation" does not apply.

We have not spoken of one of the most familiar of plant movements—that of the sensitive plant (*Mimosa pudica*). As is well known, a touch is enough to make the leaves of this plant suddenly assume their sleep position. This is usually referred to a change in a cushion of cells at the base of the leaf. Even Darwin did not think of explaining it as connected with circumnutation, although he justly regards it as an extreme case of exaggeration of the sleep movements. Its outward or bionomic utility we cannot fathom, still less its inner mechanism. It is tempting to correlate it with that remarkable "intercellular continuity of the protoplasm" which has been discovered in the tissue of this cushion—at least so far as propagation of impulse is concerned, for contractility of the network cannot be assumed. The most recent theory on the matter is that of Professor Haberlandt, who by means of very careful anatomical researches has been led to conclude that the stimulus travels down a continuous set of tubular conducting cells included in the bast portion of the leaf-strands. He believes that the transmission depends upon changes of hydrostatic pressure induced in the tubular cells and on resulting movements of the cell-sap; in other words, that it is not due to any particular nervous excitability of the living matter. But anatomical researches alone cannot justify such a conclusion; nor is it easy to see how to prove or disprove it by direct experiment.

The movements of the tentacles of the Sun-dew, of the leaves of Dionæa, of the irritable stamens of the Rockrose (Helianthemum), Barberry, etc., the closure of the stigma lips of a Mimulus upon a pollen-grain, the bending of a tendril when touched, are also to be distinguished from that series of movements to the discussion of which this chapter has been devoted; and no doubt reserve a wide and varied field for a future generation of subtle experimentalists. For instead of the animal world alone possessing movement, and the plant standing passive, the phenomena of plant movement, while of course less obvious in amount, seem to be not only the more varied in kind, but perhaps also in cause.

Summary.—The different kinds of movement may be arranged as follows:—

    A. *Movements of Growing Parts*—

        (1) "Spontaneous" movements—that is to say those whose conditions are not known, *e.g.* the revolving

movements of twiners and climbers, young shoots and roots, etc.

(2) Movements in relation to external influences:

    (*a*) Downward movement of roots and upward movement of stems.

    (*b*) Light-seeking and light-avoiding movements, especially of stems and leaves.

    (*c*) The movement of roots towards the greatest moisture.

B. *Movements of Adult Parts* —

(1) "Spontaneous" movements, *e.g.* of *Desmodium* or *Hedysarum gyrans*.

(2) Movements in relation to external influences:

    (*a*) In relation to light — sleep movements of leaves.

    (*b*) In relation to chemical and physical stimuli other than light, *e.g.* the movements of the Sensitive plant and of Fly-Traps.

Mr. Francis Darwin's Discussion of Plant Movements. — At this point it is appropriate that we should turn to what Mr. Francis Darwin, who collaborated with his father in writing *The Power of Movement in Plants*, has recently said in his Presidential address to the biological section of the British Association, 1891, which contains an important discussion of growth-curvatures, a problem towards the solution of which his detailed researches have largely contributed. A brief summary of this address, although including points already touched, may hence be of service to the student.

He begins by distinguishing the two main questions: —

1. "How does the plant recognise the vertical line; how does it know where the centre of the earth is?" — a question of irritability.

2. "In what way are curvatures which bring the plant into the vertical line executed?"—a question of the mechanism of movement.

The history of the answers to these questions may conveniently begin with Hofmeister's researches (1859) on the effects of bending or striking a turgescent shoot. He showed that when a shoot is violently bent the elasticity of the passive tissues (cortical and vascular constituents) on the convex side is injured by over-stretching. "The system must assume a new position of equilibrium; the turgescent pith (the active or erectile tissue) stretches the cortex; but as the passive tissues are now no longer equally resisting on the two sides, the shoot must assume a curvature towards that side on which the passive tissues are most resisting." Applying the same conception to a cell, Francis Darwin says: "As pith is to cortex, so is cell-pressure to cell-membrane."

When a shoot is laid horizontally there is, according to Hofmeister, a tendency for the resisting passive tissue along the lower side to become water-logged, and therefore more extensible. Therefore the shoot bends upwards. So Knight, in 1806, supposed that roots penetrated downwards, because of the sinking downwards of the juices. But both these explanations are crude; they are too mechanical.

As far back as 1824, Dutrochet, who was, however, by no means consistent, had recognised the fundamental biological fact that growth-curvatures were provoked by external influences acting as stimuli, but "the botanical mind took more than fifty years to assimilate Dutrochet's view."

In 1868 Frank attacked the problem with true physiological insight, showing that earth-seeking is an active curvature, and that it depends, like other growth-curvatures, on unequal distribution of longitudinal growth. Moreover, his experiments on the horizontal runners of the strawberry, and those of Elfving on rhizomes "paved the way for the theory that there are a variety of different organisations (or, as we now say, irritabilities) in growing plants; and that, whether a plant grows vertically upwards, or downwards, or horizontally, depends on the individual and highly sensitive constitution of the plant in question." Frank's views were, as we have seen, accepted by the authors of *The Power of Movement in Plants*, although Frank's particular interpretation of the irritabilities as due to "polarities" was not.

Francis Darwin then points out how the development of our present views on irritability was delayed by the insufficient theory of light-seeking, as implied, for instance, in De Candolle's explanation, that curvature towards the light was simply due to the more rapid growth of the shaded side. Fuller acquaintance with the facts, *e.g.* of plants which curve away from the light, showed that this again too mechanical theory was insufficient, and led on to the idea, repeatedly expressed in *The Power of Movement*, that light and gravitation act merely as landmarks by which the plant can direct itself. Pfeffer, Sachs, and Vines, and other botanical physiologists are at one in regarding growth-curvatures as phenomena of irritability, as responses to gravitation, light, and other stimuli.

So far the general question of irritability. Mr. Darwin then proceeds to discuss that of mechanism.

"The first step in advance of Hofmeister's views was the establishment of the fact that the curvatures under consideration are due to unequal growth — that is to say, to greater longitudinal growth on the convex than on the concave side." Frank made important contributions to the subject, and Sachs thoroughly demonstrated that the convex side grows faster, while the concave side grows slower, than if the organ had remained vertical and uncurved.

"Then it began to be established, through Sachs's work (1871), that turgescence is a necessary condition of growth." "De Vries (1879) maintained that growth-curvatures in multicellular organs are due to increased cell-pressure on the convex side: the rise in hydrostatic pressure being put down to increase of osmotic substances in the cell-sap of the tissues in question." But, as Francis Darwin points out, there are many serious objections to this explanation.

Many suggestions followed. Sachs directed attention to the changes in the extensibility of cell-walls. "Wiesner held that the curvature of multicellular organs is due both to an increase of osmotic force on the convex side, and to increased ductility of the membranes of the same part." "Strasburger suggested that growth-curvatures are due to increased ductility of the convex membranes."

More detailed explanations in similar lines are those of Noll and Wortmann, which differ in this: "The former lays the greater stress on the increased extensibility of the convex side, the latter on the diminution of that of the concave side. Again, Wortmann explains the difference in extensibility as due to differences in thickness of the cell-walls. Noll gives no mechanical explanation, but assumes that the outer layer of protoplasm has the power of producing changes in the quality of the cell-wall in some unknown way."

Francis Darwin concludes "there is a focussing of speculation from many sides in favour of 'active' surface-growth, or, what is perhaps a better way of putting it, in favour of the belief that the extension of cell-membranes depends on physiological rather than physical properties, that it is in some way under the immediate control of the protoplasm." Beyond that we may choose between rival suggestions of Wiesner, Strasburger, Wortmann, Noll, Vines, and others.

In the last section of his Presidential address Mr. Francis Darwin states his position in regard to circumnutation. He cites the most important criticism of *The Power of Movement*, that of Wiesner, who denied that circumnutation was a widespread phenomenon; that some stems, leaves, etc., grow in a perfectly straight line; that such curvatures as those of geotropism and heliotropism cannot be interpreted as modifications of circumnutation.

Yet, for reasons given, Mr. Francis Darwin confesses that he "cannot give up the belief in circumnutation as a widely-spread phenomenon, even though it may not be so general as was supposed." He adopts Vöchting's conception of "rectipetality"—"a regulating power leading to growth in a straight line," and says, "The essence of the matter is this: we know from experiments that a power exists of correcting excessive unilateral growth artificially produced; is it not probable that normal growth is similarly kept in an approximately straight line by a series of aberrations and corrections? If this is so, circumnutation and rectipetality would be different aspects of the same thing."

"A bicycle cannot be ridden at all unless it can 'wobble,' as every rider knows who has allowed his wheel to run in a frozen rut. In the same way it is possible that some degree of circumnutation is correlated with growth, owing to the need of regular pauses in growth. Rectipetality would thus be a power by which irregularities, inherent in growth, are reduced to order and made subservient to rectilinear growth. Circumnutation would be the outward and visible sign of the process."

Phases of Botany, Pre-Hellenic to Neo-Hellenic.— Hence, whatever detailed value be retained by the special theories of Darwin, the world will always owe him thanks; for his books have a deeper use and significance. To the dawning intelligence of the race, the forest is vaguely astir with a life which man does not clearly separate from his own — a mystery of growth which has left its mark deep in the history of all religions. A later and more self-conscious mind moulds this omnipresent life into anthropomorphic shapes; so a Dryad hides in every tree, while Pan roams through the glade. These anthropomorphic shapes are next formalised away from the living realities they symbolise; they become mere shadowy gods, then fairies and fables. The tree (or what remains of it) is now something economically useful; it has also a popular and a systematic name; but to Utilitarian or Linnæan alike, the form and substance seems the main thing, not the life. "Great Pan is dead"; the botanist is as prosaic and unseeing as the woodcutter, in fact essentially is one, at best with finer tools, and like him does his best work away from the wild wood altogether. But as the ages of fetishism, of Hellenic anthropomorphism passed away, so now the formal and utilitarian and analytic spirit is passing also in its turn. Science is entering a new and brighter Hellas; the Dryad, living and breathing, moving and sensitive is again within her tree; nay better, the plant is herself the living Dryad, her naked beauty radiant in the sun. And what of this old naturalist who led us back into the forest sounding with the Protean mystery-play of evolving Life? Now that his rugged face has vanished, it grows more strange yet more familiar in memory; we have seen it of old — we know it now for the returning avatar of Pan.

CHAPTER VI

THE WEB OF LIFE

Struggle among Plants — Perched Plants or Epiphytes — Parasitic Plants — Mistleto — Dodder — Root-Parasites — Toothwort — Broom-rapes — Saprophytes — Parasitic Fungi — Bacteria — Symbiosis.

Struggle among Plants. — In our study of climbing plants we saw that plants as well as animals had difficulties to contend with, and that there was, especially in crowded places, a more or less intense struggle for existence.

Of this the tropical forest of our frontispiece is a supreme illustration. To rise out of the perpetual twilight of their depths is a condition of success, and thus we have first tall straight-stemmed trees, then twiners and climbers which strangle and overshadow these, while strange high-perched epiphytes and parasites grow and scatter their seed over the whole tangled roof of verdure. Describing "the struggle for life in the forest," Mr. James Rodway writes of a scene in British Guiana: "We can almost fancy the magnificent forest tree protesting strongly, as octopus-like, the Clusia begins to compress and strangle it. . . . The Clusia grows stronger and stronger, until by and by, as the strangler opens its magnificent waxy flowers to the sun, and glories in its conquest, the poor unfortunate victim droops and dies. Then the trunk becomes diseased, wood ants begin their work, and finally nothing is left but the hollow cylinder of the strangler."

In the crowded vegetation by the river-side, in the meadow, along the hedgerows, the same struggle for standing room, for air, for light, must occur, and there are many peculiarities of plants which find partial explanation as adaptations of structure which help plants in crowded places to keep their foothold.

When we remember that plants have not such diverse needs as animals have; that they all require very nearly the same kind of food; that most of them get this in precisely the same way—by their roots from the soil, by their leaves from the air—we feel that there must be what may be called struggle or competition between them when they grow crowded together. We get a vivid impression of struggle for space in the crowded rosettes of a patch of house-leeks (Sempervivums), which have been allowed to grow for some time as they list; we see the younger plants budding from their parents, rising upon their shoulders, and often not only smothering them, but soon coming to crowd upon each other and compete anew. Again, only a fraction of the seedlings which appear above the surface in a plot of ground reach maturity. There is neither room nor food for them all, and the less fit are eliminated. And this is recognised practically by every farmer or gardener, for does he not thin his turnips or onions, knowing that thus alone can he ensure the success of individuals?

No doubt there is some danger of exaggerating this struggle for existence among plants, and yet more of attributing to it results which may have some entirely different origin. Experiment is much needed to substantiate what is often assumed.[1] But on general grounds

[1] A careful statement of facts was given by Mr. Walter Gardiner in

it seems much more true of plants than of animals that between those of the same kind the struggle for existence in a crowded area is very keen. For plants cannot migrate nor combine in mutual aid; in a crowd the slightly weaker must be smothered.

In this matter Darwin is again ready for us with exact observation and experiment. "From observations which I have made it appears that the seedlings suffer most from germinating in ground already thickly stocked with other plants.... The more vigorous plants gradually kill the less vigorous, though fully-grown plants; thus out of twenty species growing on a little plot of mown turf (3 feet by 4) nine species perished, from the other species being allowed to grow up freely.... Seedlings also are destroyed in vast numbers by various enemies; for instance, on a piece of ground 3 feet long and 2 wide, dug and cleared, and where there could be no choking from other plants, I marked all the seedlings of our native weeds as they came up, and out of 357 no less than 295 were destroyed, chiefly by slugs and insects."

Perched Plants or Epiphytes. — In temperate climates the only perched plants are those mosses and lichens which sometimes clothe the stems and branches of trees, but in tropical countries many Orchids, Aroids, and other flowering plants have this habit. Entirely isolated from the ground, and yet not parasitic on their bearers, how do they live? In part, of course, like other green plants, on the air and the power of the sunlight; and it is interesting to notice that they flourish best on trees, such as Cassia and Cæsalpinia, whose crown of branches is in the dry season bereft of leaves. For water and mineral matters the

a lecture entitled "How Plants maintain themselves in the Struggle for Existence," delivered at Newcastle, September 1889. See abstract in *Nature*, September 1889.

perched plants depend on the rain and damp atmosphere, for absorbing which the skin of the roots is often specially adapted, forming a kind of sponge. And although the roots do not come into contact with the soil, it seems that in some cases they may absorb salts from the decaying bark of their bearers, or from such debris as may gather about the branches.

From the great Cypress swamps of Florida, or the small but better known surviving fragment of one of these which surrounds the palace-citadel of Chapultepec, the favourite morning ride of every visitor to the city of Mexico, the traveller brings back a unique impression of mournful picturesqueness. The sombre coniferous foliage is draped with long silver-gray streamers, the "Spaniards' beards" (*Tillandsia usneoides*), one of the most conspicuous and widely distributed examples of the perching habit. This has not even roots, but fastens itself to its bearer by means of its long thread-like stems, the scales of which seem to absorb the necessary supply of water. Aroids of the genus *Philodendron*, often cultivated in our greenhouses, and Orchids belonging to the genera Dendrobium, Oncidium, Phagus, etc., are also good examples of epiphytes provided with aerial roots, which absorb water-vapour from the moist atmosphere of the tropical forest. Here indeed is the solution of a mystery which has often puzzled the botanist: how transpiration from the leaves could go on without any apparent source of water-supply. A microscopic section of the root, however, shows a tissue of characteristically thickened cell-walls, which take up moisture from the vapour-laden atmosphere during the coolness of night.

The best general account of Epiphytes is that given by Gœbel in his valuable *Pflanzenbiologische Schilderungen* (Part I., Marburg, 1889). With this Schimper's *Epiphy-*

tische Vegetation Amerikas (Jena, 1888) should be compared. Gœbel discusses, for instance, the various ways

FIG. 5.—Elk's-horn fern (*Platycerium grande*). (After Burbidge.)

in which the epiphyte effects attachment to its bearer, usually by a special disc with root-suckers, somewhat similar to that in mistletos. The spongy rind of Aroids and Orchids is regarded as primarily an organ of assimilation, but as a secondary function it absorbs moisture. Sometimes, as in *Tillandsia usneoides*, the leaves absorb water through their surface, and then the roots tend to disappear. Another fact of much interest, represented in most collections, but which Gœbel describes in detail, is the manner in which some epiphytes, especially ferns, *e.g.* "the bird's-nest fern" (*Asplenium nidus-avis*) and the "stag's-horn fern" (*Platycerium*), gather nests of humus about their roots, thus literally making soil for themselves upon the branches.

Parasitic Plants.—The perched plants which grow on the shoulders of their fellows naturally suggest parasites, which to a greater or less extent live at the expense of their hosts. As among animals, there are endoparasites, like some bacteria and fungi, which live within their hosts, and ectoparasites, which, though vitally fixed to their hosts, live outside of them.

Let us begin with the ectoparasites—the outside hangers-on. Some of these, *e.g.* the mistleto, are only in part dependent on their hosts, the parts which do not pierce the host retaining the ordinary powers of green plants; others, *e.g.* the adult dodder, are wholly dependent upon their hosts for the sustenance of their life.

Mistleto.—Of all parasitic plants the mistleto is probably most familiar, as certainly also one of the most remarkable. The species (*Viscum album*) which grows in Britain and throughout Europe is a parasite on a great variety of trees, such as apple, pear, sycamore, lime, but its favourite host is the black poplar (*Populus nigra*), and one of its rarest, in Britain at least, the oak. The strange habit of the plant, the beautiful harmony of colour between stem, leaves, and berries, its verdant and fruit-laden conspicuousness at the turn of the year towards lengthening days and summer, of which the joyous celebration by the northern peoples underlies the festival of Christmas, have made the mistleto a favourite with men; and, whether it be the sacred plant of the Druids or no, it has become the centre of many beautiful myths and customs.

A word for the life-history of the plant. In autumn and winter the white seeds are eaten by birds, especially by thrushes, and passing undigested from the food-canal are voided on the branches, to the sides of which they eventually adhere. A tree in the botanic garden at Bonn is thus specially noticeable; its trunk crowded with seedling mistletos just below a mass of branches whose sheltering attractiveness is well marked by the remains of yearly nests. From the seed a little root grows out, bends towards the branch, sticks to it, and expands into a clinging disc. From this there grows a modified rootlet which pierces the bark and reaches the wood. There is no further growth that year. But next spring the growth of new wood encloses the rootlet, which at the same time increases in length. In the second year the rootlet gives off lateral branches which grow longitudinally between the wood and the outer rind, and give off other rootlets. In proportion to the number of these the mistleto plant flourishes in stem and leaves. From the spreading roots fresh stems may arise, so that from one seed a score of mistleto bunches may arise. The rootlets penetrate into the wood and absorb what that contains — namely, as we shall afterwards see, water and salts, — while the mistleto stem spreads forth its leaves, and behaves in regard to the light and air as any independent green plant. It is in fact a natural graft.

Resembling our mistleto in most respects are other species of the same genus Viscum, the American mistleto often called by a different generic name, the more shrubby *Loranthus europæus* common on oaks and other trees in many parts of the south of Europe. There are about three hundred species of mistleto-like plants included in the order Loranthaceæ, while the genus Henslowia — plants of similar habit found in Southern Asia and in the Indian Archipelago — belongs to the order Santalaceæ.

It is interesting to notice that some of these mistleto-like plants are sometimes parasitic on one another. Thus our mistleto may grow on *Loranthus europæus*, or one species of Viscum or of Loranthus may grow on another; indeed the common mistleto has been noticed — as is natural and perhaps common enough — thus sprouting upon itself.

Dodder. — The dodders (*Cuscuta*) are parasites on such plants as clover, flax, nettles, and hops. It is on the two last that the commonest European species (*C. europæa*) is usually found. In many ways it differs from the mistleto; thus the seed almost always germinates on the ground, and the adult plant is practically destitute of chlorophyll and leaves.

Let us follow the life-history of the common dodder. Like most of the other species, it is an annual, dying away in autumn. Before that, however, the seeds have burst explosively from the seed-boxes, and have been swept hither and thither by the wind. All through the winter they lie dormant on the ground, sheltered in many cases by decaying leaves, which supply a suitable bed for germination. This does not take place till comparatively late in the following year, not before the nettles and hops have acquired some strength of stem, — a delay which is obviously of advantage to the dodder.

Out of the seed there comes a little club-shaped root which seeks the soil, but the young stem remains surrounded by the seed-husks and the store of nutriment which these enclose. It grows — thin as a thread, and somewhat spirally — at the expense of the seed-store. This is soon exhausted and growth practically stops, but the thin stem still circumnutates in sweeping circles, as if seeking about for some plant on which to cling. If this be not found, the stem at length lies prostrate on the ground, and after a strange dormant existence for a month or so longer, dies. But if some plant be near at hand, the dodder stem slings itself around it after the manner of a twining plant. As soon as its stem has embraced that of its bearer — let us say a nettle or hop — it gives off attaching papillæ which penetrate the rind and bud off numerous little rootlets. These come into close connection with the bast portion of the hop or nettle stem, and thence absorb nutritive materials. Now, in all plants the vessels of the bast form the channels by which the complex organic substances manufactured in the leaves pass towards the root. Such are the spoils which the leafless dodder, unable to manufacture organic stuffs for itself, absorbs from its host. After suitable attachment has been effected the stem continues its twining growth with increased vigour, the basal part dies away and all connection with the soil is lost, and eventually the wan parasite bursts into flower.

Root-Parasites. — In some well-shaded part of the wood we may find a large patch of the cow-wheat (*Melampyrum*) a delicate plant with a pale yellow flower, akin to toadflax and snapdragon. If we dig it up very carefully along with the plants growing near, we may be able to see that its roots are at intervals tightly bound to those of its neighbours. The connection is a vital one, and effected by peculiarly modified discs which grow round the roots of other plants and send suckers into them. This is a clear case of root-parasitism, but it is difficult to tell how much it amounts to, for the cow-wheat has also independent roots which absorb water, salts, and probably decaying vegetable matter from the soil, and it also is a green plant. If this habit were peculiar to the cow-wheat we should not be inclined to attach much importance to it, but it is far otherwise. What is true of Melampyrum is true of several hundred species of plants, especially of the orders Santalaceæ and Rhinanthaceæ. Thus the louseworts (Pedicularis) have very long surface-roots which attach themselves to the fibrous roots of the grasses and other plants of pastures and meadows. The length of the roots is in part explained, as Kerner points out, by the fact that most species of Pedicularis persist from year to year. For when a root has fixed itself to that of an adjacent annual, and that has died, it becomes necessary for the parasitic root to shift its anchorage and to find another farther on. This case of Pedicularis is further interesting because the root-hairs which are borne by the roots of most plants are here absent, except at those points where parasitic attachment is effected; not but that the skin of the root may without root-hairs absorb water and salts and the products of decaying vegetable-mould.

Of the Alpine Bartsia (*B. alpina*), Kerner states that some of the roots are parasitic, while others are adapted for absorbing humus; and among the same group of root-parasites we have also to include the odd-flowered and fruited yellow-rattles (*Rhinanthus crista-galli*), and even the pretty Eyebright or Euphrasy (*Euphrasia officinalis*) of our moorland pastures and roadsides.

The root-parasites are often blamed for spoiling pastures, and even the milk of the cattle that graze there. They certainly often occur in great abundance, and hence must to some extent impoverish the plants whose roots they suck; as yet, however, there is no definite evidence of appreciable damage done.

One wonders what constitutional peculiarity distinguishes the members of these two orders (Rhinanthaceæ and Santalaceæ), so many members of which have this strange habit of root-parasitism. Some hints of an answer have been discovered by Professor Bonnier, who finds that in Euphrasia, Bartsia, and Rhinanthus (though not in Melampyrum and some others), respiration predominates over assimilation (see chap. ix.), the oxygen which is liberated in assimilation being completely masked by the absorption of oxygen in respiration — the very reverse of that gaseous interchange characteristic of the daily life of ordinary green plants.

The Toothwort. — One of the strangest British plants is the toothwort (*Lathræa squamaria*), which has been already mentioned at chap. ii. p. 35. It lives an almost completely underground life upon the roots of poplars, hazels, and other trees, hidden by a growth of ivy, or by a heap of mouldering leaves. No young botanist will ever forget his first finding of the strange pale plant, nor can an old one ever lose his feeling of wonder as he digs down from the thick drooping spike, with its faded lilac-tinged flowers, to the still stranger underground stem, close-set with thick sharp-edged white teeth, more like a witch's necklace of human incisors than a leafy shoot. The plant, though never abundant, has a wide distribution in Europe and Asia. When we bare the thin roots which spring from the underground stem, we see that they are clasped by small adhesive discs to the roots of the tree at whose base the plant grows. From these adhesive discs, which in another European species (*Lathræa clandestina*) are about the size of split peas, suckers penetrate the tree-roots, from which without doubt the toothwort steals not only its salts and water, but the abundant starch reserves which help to swell its crowded leaves. Nor does the odd story of life end here; for each tooth-leaf has a strange recess, no mere hollow of decay, but a normal cavity, narrow of entrance, gland-lined, difficult of interpretation save as an insect trap, as which it is commonly regarded, carrying back our thoughts to the terrestrial species of Utricularia (p. 31). Few botanists imagine that this strange and local plant may be cultivated; it grows well under cherry laurels ("common bay," *Cerasus laurocerasus*) in the shrubberies of the Edinburgh Botanic Garden, and hence at least suggests the possibility of its introduction elsewhere.

Broom-rapes. — In our search for the toothwort we may perhaps find one of the broom-rapes (*Orobanche*), which grow parasitically on the roots of thyme, scabious, and other common plants. As in Lathræa, there is no chlorophyll; but the union between parasite and host is much more intimate, so much so indeed that it is difficult to separate them, or to tell where the tissues of the parasite end and those of the host begin. The seedling of the broom-rape and related parasites is very remarkable; it bears no trace of cotyledons, but is a delicate thread-like structure, one end of which is hidden by the remains of the seed, while the other grows in search of roots to which to fix itself. If these be not soon found, the seedling shrivels and dies, for it seems quite unable to absorb food from the soil. But if a suitable host be found, the seedling becomes ultimately united with it, thickening into a knotted tuber-like structure, from which the flower-bearing stem with its brown useless leaves will afterwards rise above the ground.

Thus from the non-parasitic toad-flax and its allies, which we shall come to know better as the natural order *Scrophulariaceæ*, commonly gay flowered and free growing, often indeed mischievous as weeds, we have a regular gradation through cow-wheat and Euphrasy, lousewort and Bartsia, to full parasites like toothwort and broom-rape. For still further modified allies of the broom-rapes (Orobanche) we must travel abroad, especially to tropical countries, where there are many strange plants (Balanophoreæ) of similar habit but strangely crowded and reduced flowers.

Best known among these, especially to tradition, is the odd *Cynomorium*, a plant of fungus-like appearance, long known as *Fungus melitensis*. It is found in the islands of Malta and Gozo, and is remarkable for its scarlet colour and blood-like juice, which, according to the "doctrine of signatures," were interpreted as providential indications of its value as a cure for all diseases accompanied by bleeding. Even stranger are the Rafflesias, found in the Indian islands and in South America. They have neither a developed stem nor leaves, but are reduced practically to a flower closely fixed to the roots of some other plant (usually a species of Cissus). The largest species, discovered in 1818 in Sumatra by Dr. Arnold, and sent by Sir Thomas Stamford Raffles to Robert Brown, who hence gratefully named it Rafflesia Arnoldi, measures about a yard in diameter, and is, one need hardly say, the largest of all known flowers. It seems, however, a repulsive giant, fleshy and fungus-like, coarse and gaudy, worst of all, fetid as carrion, and hence swarming with appropriate insects, who even lay their eggs in preparation for its foul decay, and so, too, doubtless render the service of fetching and carrying pollen from flower to flower.

Saprophytes. — A large number of plants, especially in the woods, some with and some without chlorophyll, depend in great part at least on the abundant organic material afforded by the decaying leaves and other parts of plants — in other words, on the humus or vegetable mould of the soil. This is true, for instance, of the Bird's-nest Orchis (*Neottia nidus-avis*), of the rootless *Corallorhiza*, of the little twæ-blade (*Listera cordata*), and of many other orchids. But it is very difficult to draw any hard and fast line between parasites, which live on living organisms, and the so-called saprophytes, which live on decaying organic matter. Thus the species of cow-wheat (Melampyrum) and yellow rattle (Rhinanthus), which are undoubtedly root-parasites, appear also to depend upon the humus of the soil; the ~~death~~ *Monotropa Hypopitys* is said to be a parasite in the pine woods, but a saprophyte on the rotting leaves under other trees; and some of the epiphytes gather so many decaying leaves around their roots that it is likely that some of them should also be called saprophytes. The staghorn-fern (Platycerium), so commonly grown as a suspended ornament of our greenhouses, may here again be an instructive case (see p. 99).

Parasitic Fungi. — Of infinitely greater importance as mischief-makers in the world than the parasitic flowering plants are the innumerable parasitic Fungi. Those which cause mildew, potota-disease, some diseases of cereals, vine-plants, and timber-trees, and so on, are often disastrous to the prosperity of a fertile region, nay, as modern experience as well as history too often tells, to a province, a whole nation. Nor do they affect plants alone, but also animals, and even man himself; witness respectively salmon-disease and ringworm.

Fungi being, like dodder, toothwort, and broom-rape, plants without any chlorophyll, they are unable to use the carbonic acid gas of the air, as green plants do, and are therefore dependent upon ready-made supplies of organic matter. Hence we find them living either as parasites on living plants and animals, or as saprophytes on decaying organisms, or in some cases indifferently on either.

As we do not propose here to do more than indicate the part played by fungi in the economy of nature, either in destroying living organisms or in utilising the products of decay, we refer the student to that convenient and interesting introduction to the subject supplied by Professor Marshall Ward in his little volume on *Timber and some of its Diseases* (Nature Series, Lond. 1889), and for systematic information to the text-book of *Cryptogamic Botany*, by Bennett and Murray (Lond. 1889). As an easy introduction to the subject, the writer's article "Fungi" in *Chambers's Encyclopædia* may in the first place be read.

Bacteria. — Of all parasitic plants, the smallest — the microscopic Bacteria — are the most important. It is true that not all of them are parasitic, for many live in rottenness, but they all agree in being minute colourless units unable to live, as green plants do, on water, salts, carbonic acid, and sunlight; able to thrive only when they find organic substances of some sort ready-made for them.

We have already seen that their presence may help to explain the disappearance of flies within the traps of some of the insectivorous plants, and we can detect the work of bacteria in a hundred ways all around us. If we leave a piece of meat or fish (whether cooked or raw matters not) in an open vessel filled with clear water, this becomes turbid, and a scum gathers on the surface; if we examine this scum under a high power of the microscope we see incalculable numbers of bacteria. On the other hand, if the piece of meat be placed in a glass flask which is filled with water, then boiled for a short time, and carefully closed, while still boiling, with a plug of cotton-wool, the water will remain quite clear, and the flesh will not decompose. The only difference between the two cases is that in the latter the bacteria in the water have been killed by boiling, and are kept out of the flask by the cotton-wool, therefore we may say that the decomposition observed in the first case was due to bacteria. So it is always. As Huxley in aphoristic style puts it, "Putrefaction is the result not of death, but of life."

It is more than two centuries since the keen-eyed Leeuwenhoek — that early devotee of the microscope to whom, despite his rude and feeble instruments, the most abundant laurels of discovery must be awarded — discovered this living dust, a knowledge of which has not only changed some of our biological conceptions and created the dominant school of medical theorists, but reformed and rationalised surgery and hygiene, and exercised a potent influence upon the greatest industries. To what is the importance of bacteria due? They are very minute, quite invisible individually to our unaided eyes — minute spheres, rods, or spirals they are, the smallest unit masses of living matter. The secret of their strength is in their power of multiplication. By repeated division and redivision one soon becomes a thousand; indeed, given sufficient food, in a few hours a single unit may have become the progenitor of millions.

But their importance depends also on their universal distribution. Universal, indeed, for they live in the air and in the soil, in food and raiment, in man, in beast, in plant; not even the water which we drink is free from them. From the mouths of men to the walls of their houses and the flies on the windows, from the hair of the head to the toes of the feet, from the highway dust to the recesses of the forest, and from wayside pool to sea, bacteria abound. But while they spread here, there, and everywhere, they become most obvious wherever dead organic matter is abundant, as in the refuse of our towns, or in dead plants and animals. Rancid butter and rotten cheese, "high" game-flavoured meats and over-stale bread, blue milk and soured wine, as well as cesspools and dust-heaps, sewers and slums, are their common habitats.

Most important, however, is the fact expressed in the "germ-theory," that bacteria are constantly and intimately associated with some of the most fatal of human diseases, such as consumption, diphtheria, smallpox or typhoid, malaria or leprosy. Bacteria, in fact, kill most of us.

multiplying within us so as to choke the system, at once feeding greedily on the tissues or fluids of the body, and poisoning us in every cell with the waste-products of their loathsome life. It would take us too far from present botanical considerations to discuss the ways in which we are saved from the bacteria which so easily beset us. There are happily many drugs and reagents of inward or outward use, from quinine to carbolic acid, and all the other ever-multiplying antiseptics — drugs which they cannot stomach. Like the Acacia tree with its bodyguard of ants driving off other dangerous ants, so, some tell us, we may have a protective standing army of bacteria which save us from others; at all events, the widely accepted theory of Metschnikoff makes us view the animal body as garrisoned by the uncoloured blood-corpuscles or leucocytes which seize the intruding microbes just as amœbæ would do, and digest them beyond the reach of mischief. But when the germs become too numerous or the warders enfeebled, the bacterial parasite begins its growth, and the disease has set in. Such, for instance, Dr. Gulland tells us, is the use of the tonsils which lie on either side of the pharynx; in health they furnish a continual succession of these corpuscle sentries, while in the inflammations to which they are so subject, the bacteria have been too many, the defence too weak. This subject is at present under active controversy, not a few bacteriologists maintaining that the germicidal virtues of the blood lie wholly or mainly in the serum, not in the corpuscles.

But the most potent preventive, universal and costless, is a natural one — the sunlight. Miquel, of the excellent bacteriological observatory of the Parc Montsouris at Paris, and several French bacteriologists have shown that the sun's light, even without the heat, for a few bright hours is able to kill the germs which float in the air, and leave them harmless. What it requires hard boiling to accomplish, the sunlight does with rapid ease. For although the spores or young bacteria which are carried in the air are peculiarly hardy, able to nurse their dormant virulence for months or even years, ready when they find a suitable resting-place to multiply with appalling swiftness, they cannot withstand the power of the sunlight. What is the light of life to other plants, is to the bacteria death. Perhaps it makes them live for a short time so rapidly that their scanty speck of living substance is worn out and consumed beyond possibility of repair. Quite literally then "the pestilence walketh in darkness." Hence then we may interpret much of the history of disease, and see that we have here no mere mysterious visitations, to be crouched before with submissive dread; but a definite and intelligible part of the order of nature not only to be analysed and grasped by science, but which we may partly modify by art and partly by adapting our other conditions. And thus it is that we find so many dead germs in the air; thus we regard all dark places as evil, whether they be the lidless coffins of the slums or the dungeon-like sunk flats of west-end houses; thus we begin to appreciate the hygienic importance of sunlight—the most universal, the most economical, the most potent antagonist of our subtlest and deadliest foes.

But the part which bacteria play in the economy of nature is often beneficent. For although we may not derive much satisfaction from the fact that bacteria by thinning out the weaker organisms help to keep up the standard of vitality, a little observation leaves the more cheering conviction that many of them are among the great cleansers of the world. Out of dead plants some form vegetable mould, while others reduce the carcases of animals to simpler and purer substances. Consider the large circle on which bacteria occupy an arc; green plants feed on air, water, and the salts of the soil; many animals feed upon plants, even the most purely carnivorous are of course indirectly dependent upon them; dead animals are consumed by bacteria, which in so doing set free carbonic acid gas and ammonia, which steal off into the air, and nitrates and the like which soak down into the soil, all to be utilised by the plant-world anew. Here then the bacteria furnish the indispensable means by which the circulation of the materials of organic life is perpetually renewed.

In this connection we may appropriately discuss an interesting story in regard to the relations between bacteria and some other plants. Pull up a bean-plant, wash gently and examine the roots. Here and there may be noted small rounded swellings or tubercles, sometimes as large as peas. The same may be seen on the roots of vetches and other leguminous plants, and also on some cereals. That they are not normal parts of the plants is clear, for there are roots without a trace of them; and if the seeds be grown in soil that has been calcined at a high temperature or in water that has been boiled, the tubercles are not formed. This becomes yet more evident when the tubercles are examined microscopically, for then they are seen to exhibit, not the tissues of a rootlet, but crowds of minute rod-like or somewhat spherical bodies.

What then is the meaning of the tubercles? The researches of numerous botanists, with a controversy which has been in progress since 1858, when these tubercles were first noted, have at length convinced most of us that the little rod-like bodies contained in the tubercles are bacteria, and that the tubercles are due to the infection of the plants by these micro-organisms. As to their physiological effect on the plant, the investigators are not yet thoroughly agreed, but the conclusions of Hellriegel and Willfarth, corroborated by some others, are of great interest. By growing leguminous plants and cereals in calcined earth and with a supply of water that has been boiled, they obtained plants without tubercles on their roots; by watering these with water which has been in contact with the soil in which tubercled roots have grown, they were able to infect the plants, or they could also inoculate them directly. After infection or inoculation the plants acquire a new vigour, and they increase in nitrogenous substances to a greater extent than can be accounted for by the nitrogenous salts in the soil. To explain this it seems necessary to believe that with the help of their partner bacteria the legumes and cereals are able to utilise the free nitrogen of the air. If so, they are able to do what, as we shall afterwards see (chap. ix.), is regarded by most botanists as quite impossible for other plants.

Symbiosis.—Whatever be the final verdict in regard to the alleged partnership between bacteria and their leguminous or cereal hosts, there are other cases of mutually helpful partnership in regard to which there is no doubt. To this De Bary in 1879 applied the name Symbiosis (literally, a living together). It is interesting to notice the parallels among animals; zoophytes clustered on the backs of crabs are comparable to epiphytes; among animals as among plants there are many external and internal parasites; the well-known partnerships between hermit-crabs and sea-anemones are examples of the beginnings of a truly co-operative symbiosis.

The most important case of symbiosis among plants indeed by far the most fully-developed case in nature, is that of the lichens. These used of course to be regarded, as they no doubt popularly are still, as definite individual plants united by common characters into a well-marked group or "natural order," which botanists were wont to reckon along with algæ and fungi, but no less distinct than these. Their immense variety has given no small amount of labour to the systematists, and a well-developed specialism of "lichenology" with a literature and with collections voluminous enough to surprise any one who first enters upon it, has arisen in consequence. In 1866 the penetrating cryptogamist De Bary threw out the suggestion that the many resemblances shown by the lichens on one hand to fungi and on the other to algæ, might really be due to an admixture of these two constitutents. The idea was taken up and worked out carefully by his pupil Schwendener, to whose practical insight and industrial training the science owes other important ideas.

From the fungus-like tissue of a lichen he isolated little greenish cells like Protococcus and other unicellular algæ, and in some cases these green cells were able to live and multiply after they had been isolated. This remarkable fact led Schwendener to develop the hint given by De Bary, and to establish his so-called "dual hypothesis" of the nature of lichens.

"As the result of my researches," he says, "all these growths (lichens) are not simple plants, not individuals in the ordinary sense of the word; they are rather colonies consisting of hundreds and thousands of individuals, among which, however, one predominates, while the rest in perpetual captivity prepare the nutriment for themselves and their master. This master is a fungus, a parasite which is accustomed to live upon others' work; its slaves are green algæ, which it has sought out, or indeed caught hold of and compelled into its service. It surrounds them, as a spider its prey, with a fibrous net of narrow meshes, which is gradually converted into an impenetrable covering; but while the spider sucks its prey and leaves it dead, the fungus incites the algæ found in its net to more rapid activity, indeed to more vigorous increase."

The lichenologists were indignant at this proposed revolutionary demolition of their science, and defended the traditional position stoutly from 1869 to 1873; but in that year the leading algologist, M. Bornet, fully confirmed and extended the results of Schwendener, showing, for instance, that a single "lichen" might really contain three or four distinct and familar species of algæ, overrun and woven into a false tissue by a single mould; while the lichenologist's contention, that the green alga-like cells developed from the fungus-like filaments, was shown to be based on incorrect observation, the former being really only sucked by close-fitting or ingrowing protrusions of the latter. Another important proof was given by Stahl, who succeeded in making lichens artificially, *i.e.* by taking a known alga, and sowing a known fungus upon it; a lichen, a *known* lichen, was the result. How obstinately the controversy raged is oddly commemorated in the still current edition of the *Encyclopædia Britannica*; thus the article BOTANY retains the older view, while FUNGI states the modern, LICHENS (of course by an eminent and conservative lichenologist) returns to the traditional standpoint, while this is finally corrected at PARASITISM. That, however, no shadow of doubt any longer exists on the matter is well shown by the recent researches of Bonnier, who has not only repeated the synthetic experiments of Stahl with all bacteriological precautions, but varied them by substituting the protonema or filamentous alga-like stage of the life-history of a moss for the ordinary alga constituent.

Since then it is not only possible to separate the algæ constituent, and to see it live independently while the fungal one as naturally starves, but also to combine the two elements into a unified life, we believe that a lichen is not a single, but a double organism,—an intimate union of an alga and a fungus, living in mutual helpfulness or symbiosis. After we have considered the physiology of the leaf, we shall be better able to understand how really helpful the two kinds of elements which compose a lichen are to one another (see

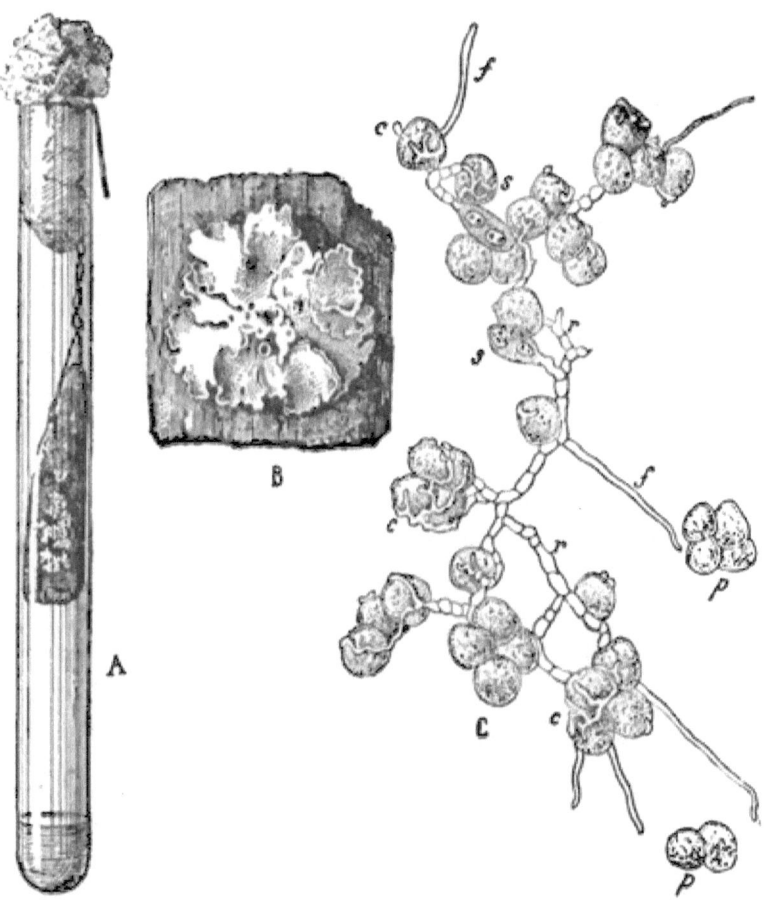

FIG. 6.— Patch of lichen grown synthetically by Bonnier (from sowing of fungus spores on algæ) under bacteriological precautions against entrance of foreign spores. (After Bonnier.)

chap. v.) Yet we already see that we have here a tiny repetition of the organic universe, of the Balance of Nature between plant and animal. The lichenologist is no real loser; if his specimen has lost its individuality, it has gained a higher and more complex one; and it is a microcosm of nature to boot.

It is also interesting to notice the existence of what Zukal calls "half-lichens," in which the mutual partnership has not been thoroughly established. For certain fungi usually occurring as lichens may, in certain conditions, live bereft of their partner-algæ, as saprophytes; while others, which are usually parasites or saprophytes, are sometimes found combined with algæ, and forming lichens. We have thus what we may fairly consider lichens in the making.

An interesting parallel to the case of lichens, in which the part of the fungus may be taken by animals of very various kinds, is that of the "yellow cells," first known as practically constant features of the organisation of the Radiolarians, and long supposed to form an essential part of these, but also occurring in the tissues of many much higher organisms, especially Cœlenterates. Notably the large sea-anemone *Anthea cereus*, which prospers and multiplies greatly in consequence. These yellow cells survive after their host dies, or even after being isolated; they divide like unicellular algæ; they contain starch, and a pigment like that of Diatoms; they have a wall of cellulose, and they evolve oxygen during sunshine. Therefore they are regarded with justice as partner algæ. As they live they remove carbonic acid and nitrogenous waste from their partners, and evolve oxygen which accelerates the vital processes of the animal; they form starch, which when dissolved passes out by exosmosis into the animal tissues; when they die they are digested. The partnership is therefore one of benefit to both parties. There has been considerable dispute as to details, but the general facts of this symbiosis between plants and animals are admitted by all.

Strasburger has discovered an interesting association

between a small aquatic plant called Azolla and one of the freshwater algæ called Anabæna. On the under surface of each floating leaf of Azolla there is a small opening leading into a cavity in the substance of the leaf. In this cavity a colony of the alga is always found. The alga may indeed live independently in the water, but the Azolla is never without its partner. We are not, however, certain as to the precise meaning of the association; and it may be doubted whether we have really here as yet any appreciable measure of true co-operation at all. Yet through such mere mechanical associations or juxtapositions true parasitism and symbiosis must largely have arisen.

One of the strangest kinds of reputed symbiosis is the occurrence of fungi around the roots of certain plants. Frank and others have shown that the root-tips of beeches, birches, hazels, and the like, are invested by a net of fungus-threads. They suggest that the net acts as a sort of sponge intermediate between the roots and the soil, and this idea of the "mycorhiza," as the fungus network is called, receives some corroberation from the fact that in heaths and some orchids the fungus-threads actually penetrate into the substance of the root. The question is, however, under hot discussion, the veteran arboriculturist, Hartig, stoutly maintaining that we have here nothing beyond a mere parasitism of the mould filaments upon the tree-roots. The controversy is one which the student may profitably follow, summarising (and where possible checking by actual observation) the arguments on either side.

CHAPTER VII

RELATIONS BETWEEN PLANTS AND ANIMALS

Plants and Snails — Plants and Ants — Domatia — Myrmecodia — Galls — Plants and Aphides — Cats and Clover.

Relations between Plants and Animals. — Our study of insectivorous plants and of plant-movements have already shown us that the conventional distinctions between plants and animals are by no means natural. Of this fundamental unity Linnæus had some conception when he united plants and animals under the common title *Organisata*, in contrast to the mineral world of matter merely aggregated, not organised, as *Conserta*, and to have demonstrated the essential unity of organic life is one of the most important characteristics of modern botany. The reader will do well to consult Claude Bernard's work, of which the title is a summary, *Sur les Phénomènes de la Vie communs aux Animaux et aux Végétaux*. Nor can it too clearly be realised that the distinctness of three kingdoms of nature, animal, vegetable, and mineral, however stereotyped in school-books, is, like much else we have learned there, a survival of mediæval non-science. It is in fact a doctrine of the alchemists, of which the whole science of biology, the whole doctrine of evolution is the confutation. How and where to divide the Organisata into *Animalia* and

Vegetabilia, with or without a common debatable land of *Protista* (or it may be a still more fundamental, albeit in its own way strangely specialised group of *Myxomycetes*), is an important controversy enough, yet after all a mere internal problem for biologists to settle among themselves.

Recognising then plants and animals as two main groups of living creatures, which in their life have to solve essentially the same problems, we may profitably continue to study the many points of contact between them, interrelations such as those which we have already described between insectivorous plants and their prey. Illustrations of these interactions are growing increasingly numerous.

The seedlings, whose struggle for existence Darwin was fond of watching, were sometimes thinned by one another, and sometimes by the weather, but often by slugs, insects, and other animals. This is of course the most obvious of relations; hosts of vegetarian animals feed upon plants. Nor is this relation so one-sided as it looks, for in so doing the animals are often of real service. The thrush which eats the mistleto-berries spreads the undigested seeds from tree to tree; the bees which rob the flowers of their nectar are at the same time the bearers of fertilising pollen from plant to plant; even the cattle which wholly eat up some kinds of herbage give others more room in which to grow.

That animals select one kind of plant and leave others untouched is an undoubted fact, and it is easy to believe that this selective process may have many important results. Let us take the case of snails and plants which was studied in great detail a few years ago by Professor Stahl,[1] the experimental lichenologist already quoted.

Plants and Snails. — There are two kinds of snails — omnivorous eaters and "specialists," as Stahl calls them. The latter are epicures, feeding daintily on toadstools and

[1] *Pflanzen und Schnecken*, 8vo. Jena, 1888.

the like; the majority, unfortunately for our gardens, will eat almost any verdure they can find. They have large appetites, able to devour an eighth part of their weight of cabbage in three hours; and as every gardener mourns, they are also very abundant; 150 have been seen around a plot of but a square yard, and an industrious naturalist in one day collected 1200 of a single species from a piece of ground three-quarters of a mile square.

But while snails, always excepting the "specialists," are not fastidious in their diet, they draw the line somewhere. Certain plants they have found do not agree with them, and these they eschew. They try them, suffer for it, remember their experience, and leave the disagreeable plants alone for the future.

Here then we have a problem such as a German professor loves, and which no one can tackle with more painstaking industry than he, — not even Darwin with his sundews, — to tempt innumerable snails with all manner of meats, to find out their favourite menu and their *index expurgatorius* of viands, and to make a theory out of it. Thus Professor Stahl enumerates at least fifteen different ways in which plants have become abhorrent to snails, and are thereby protected. Some plants are too sour, others are poisonous; some are full of ferments, others are rich in purgative oils. There may be bristling hairs which prick the sole of the snail's "foot" as it creeps on the plant; or limy and flinty armature which makes eating too slow and laborious even for a slug; or slimy secretions which prevent the animals from getting a good grip; or, best of all, the tissues may contain thousands of little crystal needles which stick in the lips and make them smart.

If you chew a little piece — let it be only a little piece — of the cuckoo-pint (*Arum maculatum*), which grows in the shady corner of the wood, your tongue and lips will be painfully excited for some time afterwards. This property is much exaggerated in some of its allies; thus the "Dumb-Cane" of the West Indies is associated with ugly tales of slave-torture, and even nowadays with occasional cruel practical joking among the usually gentle and kindly race of gardeners. Even in Arum some acrid poison is present, but the irritating effect is mainly due to the myriads of minute needle-like crystals (the *raphides* of old books on the microscope) which the plant's tissues contain, and which pierce the soft skin of the experimenter's mouth. After this experience one remembers the cuckoo-pint; can you believe that the snails, which both Darwin and Romanes credit with good memories, will forget? For years a taste or a smell will remain in the memory, and just as the suggestion of a mouthful of flinty horsetails gives one a "goose-skin" shiver, so the snail on a renewed impression of a disagreeable plant writhes its horns in disgust and turns away.

Stahl's research is doubtless valuable; it is interesting to know of the fifteen different kinds of protection which save plants from being eaten by snails, though when he says that he finds no wild flowering plant — not even a tree — without some kind of protection against snails, the suspicion cannot be repressed that he is proving a great deal too much. And when he goes on to interpret these protective qualities as being in direct relation to the appetite of snails, to credit snails with being important factors in the evolution of these qualities, we emphatically protest against his conclusion.

The notion is of course a familiar one, but the truth that there is in it may be falsely exaggerated. Something unusual happened within a plant and it became sour; the snails tasted it and left it alone, but ate up its relatives which remained sweet. These eaten up, the sour plant was left to produce other sour plants, on which the snails, this time a trifle less fastidious, have to begin anew. They naturally select the sweeter, and hence "natural selection" preserves and propagates the sourer; and so on indefinitely, and vegetation thus tends to grow sourer to all eternity. For this the snails are responsible! Meanwhile, too, natural selection, her ministers this time the browsing mammals, is at work producing thorny plants, and so on. It is the Darwinian theory in a nutshell; and its acceptance or rejection is of fundamental importance to our whole conception of evolution. Not only to Professor Stahl, therefore, but to Mr. Wallace, to Professors Weismann and Ray Lankester, perhaps even to the mildly divergent Mr. Romanes, as assuredly to Sir John Lubbock or Mr. Grant Allen, such interpretations seem not only valid but necessary, and not only necessary but sufficient.

You have two dozen apples in your fruit-basket just beginning to spoil. Each day you take the two best, and at the end of a week there are ten rotten apples left. To a slight extent, it may be said, you are responsible for the growing rottenness, for you might have periodically selected the two worst, but the rottenness was there; it not only arose, but increased without you. Your selection, it is true, has been such as to accelerate this disastrous evolution; a different selection would have retarded it; what selection can do then is at most to accelerate or slow the progress of the selected along its definite grooves of natural change. So the acids and ferments, the oils and encrustations, the hurtful hairs and crystal needles, are constitutional peculiarities which arise in plants, and increase in them apart altogether from any snails. Nature is indeed a marvellous web, but we must not make it more tangled than it is. The sourness, the poison, the ferments, the crystals, are, so to speak, "in the blood." Their occurrence is widespread, and in some cases their primary meaning in the internal economy of the plant is well known.

The idea that tannin has been developed as a protection against snails and other animal enemies is no doubt at first sight attractive, while we are ignorant of its real nature, and also while we ignore the fact that a plant rich in tannin, like the oak, may be peculiarly a prey to animal enemies, or meet it by inventing a fresh hypothesis of the adaptation of some animal enemies to withstand the defence. But when it, like the protective crystals, becomes viewed as essentially a waste product, and as therefore necessarily turned out in definite chemical proportion by the life-processes of the plant, the natural selectionist argument recedes as far into the background as it would have to do in explaining the origin of the crystalline form or taste of any chemical product, the colour of any precipitate, the lustre or specific gravity of a mineral.

We laugh at those who said, "So are fleas black that they may be caught more readily upon a white ground," but are we becoming wiser now, if it be true, as Professor Stahl thinks, and we fear only with too much justice, that the majority of modern naturalists would corroborate the opinion that the protective characters of plants stand in direct causal connection with the appetite of animals? To give snails credit for evolving plants with crystals, sourness, and poison, to make cattle and the like responsible for the thorns on plants, is like giving snakes the credit of evolving boots which protect our heels. In all these cases alike the possibility of some defensive utility is undenied, nor even of some improvement through selective agency; what is contended for is, however, a change in our evolutionary perspective, laying increased importance upon the definiteness and cumulativeness of the internal variation and consequently a diminished stress upon the external selection which plays upon this.

Hence we have all sympathy with a recent critic, Dr. Jumelle, who, in reviewing a recent endeavour to explain not only the presence but the position of alkaloids, etc., in plants by showing how defensive they are, says: "The final causes to which so many authors constantly appeal, have indeed the advantage of supplying an easy explanation of embarrassing facts, but they are hurtful to the progress of science, since the mind duped by an illusory satisfaction is dissuaded from further investigation."

Plants and Ants.—Both gardeners and botanists have long been aware that ants are among the most frequent guests of flowering plants, and such names as *Myrmecodia*, *Euphorbia formicarum*, refer to this. Are these visitors hurtful? In most cases only to a slight extent, for although they rob the flowers of honey, they compensate for this by eating other small insects which would do the plants much harm. They are useful to the plant but not to its flowers, for as the worker-ants are not winged, they are not suited for carrying the fertilising pollen from plant to plant as bees and flies often do. They devour pollen and nectar without fulfilling any useful function, and it is said that when there are crowds of them about a flower the bees are apt to have their noses somewhat rudely pulled when they thrust them into the recesses of the flower, and this will obviously tend to frighten away the bees. But without attaching much importance to this allegation that the ants assault the bees, we see that it is advantageous that the ants should be excluded from the flowers. In many plants this is effectively done. There may be, as in some of the teasel tribe, *chevaux-de-frise* of stiff, downward-pointing hairs, like those inside of a pitcher plant, against which the ants cannot climb. There may be sticky parts of the stem which the insects cannot cross, as we see in some of the catchflies, *e.g. Lychnis viscaria* and others. There may be very slippery stems on which the climbers can find no foothold, "and the flowers are often pendulous, as in snowdrop and cyclamen, creeping creatures being thus kept out of them, just as the pendulous nests of the weaver bird are a protection against snakes and other enemies." Sir John Lubbock quotes from Kerner, whose charming *Flowers and their Unbidden Guests* is most full of information on this head, the case of *Polygonum amphibium*, a common pond-weed, which, as its name suggests, lives amphibiously, sometimes in water, sometimes on land. "So long as it grows in water it is protected by the water, and its stem is smooth; but, on the other hand, those specimens which live on land throw out certain hairs, which terminate in sticky glands, and thus prevent small insects from creeping up to the flowers. In this case, therefore, the plant is not sticky, except just when this condition is useful." In many cases, too, the flowers, like those of the snapdragon, are virtually closed boxes which can be opened by the bees, but not by the small ants, unless indeed these bite a hole through the base of the petals.

But it may be asked, if the ants are excluded from the flowers in any of these ways, why do they visit the plants at all? Partly, no doubt, by way of experiment, partly for the sake of the booty of smaller insects which they find about the leaves, but also because the secretion of nectar is not always confined to the flowers, but may take place on other parts of the plant—in what are called extra-floral nectaries, of which something will afterwards be said.

But the web has another mesh. As long ago as 1688 John Ray noted the constant occurrence of ants in the hollow stems of the South American *Cecropia palmata*, and many other naturalists had called attention to the same and similar cases. But precise knowledge of the meaning of this partnership was not attained till 1874, when Belt, the naturalist of Nicaragua, and Delpino, an Italian botanist, cleared up the whole matter. Let us quote Belt's account[1] of his discovery: "The thorns of the bull's-horn Acacia are hollow, and are tenanted by ants that make a small hole for their entrance and exit near one end of the thorn, and also burrow through the partition that separates the two horns, so that one entrance serves for both. Here they rear their young, and in the wet season every one of the thorns is tenanted, and hundreds of ants are to be seen running about, especially over the younger leaves. If one of them be touched, or a branch shaken, the little ants (*Pseudomyrma bicolor*) swarm out from the hollow thorns, and attack the aggressor with jaws and sting. They sting severely, raising a little white lump that does not disappear in less than twenty-four hours. They form a most efficient standing army for the plant, which prevents not only the mammalia from browsing on the leaves, but delivers it from the attacks of a much more dangerous enemy — the leaf-cutting ant. For these services the ants are not only securely housed by the plant, but are provided with a bountiful supply of food, and to secure their attendance at the right time and place, the food is so arranged and distributed as to effect that object with wonderful perfection." There is a sweet gland at the base of each pair of leaflets on the bipinnate leaf, and a little yellow pear-like body at the end of each small division of the compound leaf which is carried off when ripe. The young thorns are soft and filled with sweet pulp, so that the ant finds its house full of food. As it hollows this out, the thorn increases in size and bulges out towards the base.

[1] *The Naturalist in Nicaragua.* Lond. 1874.

"These ants seem at first sight to lead the happiest of existences. Protected by their stings, they fear no foe. Habitations full of food are provided for them to commence housekeeping with, and cups of nectar and luscious fruits await them every day. But there is a reverse to the picture. In the dry season on the plains the acacias cease to grow. No young leaves are produced, and the old glands do not secrete honey. Then want and hunger overtake the ants that have revelled in luxury all the wet season; many of the thorns are depopulated, and only a few ants live through the season of scarcity. As soon, however, as the first rains set in, the trees throw out numerous vigorous shoots, and the ants multiply again with astonishing rapidity."

A more recent traveller, Professor A. F. W. Schimper, who has reinvestigated the whole matter, has gathered some new facts of much interest, and the student may be referred to Schimper's book [1] not only on its own account, but for the bibliography of the subject which it contains.

He tells us first of the destructive ravages of the leaf-cutting ants, the sight of whose march soon becomes familiar to the traveller in tropical America. In a minute or two a sixpence-like circle is cut from a leaf and the ant marches off with its burden. Only the dry and the very young leaves are spared, and armies of thousands of ants soon make sad havoc of a tree's foliage. It is not quite certain what the ants do with the leaves which they carry home: Bates believed that they were used as a lining for the subterranean galleries; Belt supposed that the ants fed upon fungi which grew upon the decaying leaves; M'Cook observed, in the case of *Atta fervens* and *A. septentrionalis*, that a papery material was manufactured from the leaves and used in the

---

[1] *Die Wechselbeziehungen zwischen Pflanzen und Ameisen in tropischen Amerika*, 8vo. Jena, 1888. Cp. E. Huth, *Myrmecophile und Myrmecophobe Pflanzen*. Berlin, 1887.

internal furnishing of the ant's nest; but the subject requires further investigation.

The destructive leaf-cutters have certain preferences; imported plants, such as oranges, roses, coffee-plants, and mango, are greedily attacked; Solanaceæ and grasses are left untouched, but in South Brazil Schimper found that the guava, a *Caladium, Cassia neglecta*, and *Alchornea iricurana* were peculiarly liable to be ruined. It is certain that the presence of ethereal oils and ferments is not always a deterrent to the ants, whatever it may be to snails, else orange, guava, mango, rose, etc., would not be such favourites. There can be little doubt that the leaf-cutters would soon exterminate these and other imported plants if no precautions were used, and it is likely that they have in this way exterminated many indigenous species. The leaves of the common orange and the bitter orange are eagerly used, but those of the mandarine and the lemon are avoided. Thus in the natural course of things the two first would be eliminated, the two last preserved. This may be taken as a good example of the action of natural selection, but we cannot of course ascribe to the influence of the ants the qualities which save the lemon and the mandarine.

In the province of Canton in China it is the custom to place nests of harmless, tree-inhabiting ants upon the orange-trees in order to defend these from the attacks of the leaf-cutters. This is but an intentional imitation of what has taken place in the course of nature. For, as Belt has told us, the ants which inhabit various species of *Cecropia, Cassia*, and other plants serve as a bodyguard against destructive intruders. Let us follow Schimper's account of this "symbiosis."

Schimper's problem, shortly stated, is whether the plants, which are so constantly furnished with a bodyguard of ants, exhibit structures which can be definitely regarded as adaptations due to the symbiosis. "Of late," he says, "naturalists have become more and more accustomed to interpret all structural peculiarities which are seen to be useful for a certain purpose, as if they had originated for that purpose." This Schimper rightly regards as unscientific. All such interpretations must rest on observation and experiment.

Many ants live in the nooks which plants often afford — in the axils of leaves, among the tangled roots of epiphytes, inside old galls, and so on; others build nests which they fix to the branches; others bore labyrinthine passages in the dead bark of trees. "The fanatics of biology" (*i.e.* bionomics) "are inclined to find adaptations in all such cases of constant or usual symbiosis. The chambers of *Tillandsia bulbosa*, the feltwork of aerial roots in the case of many epiphytes, the cavities of the stem and branches in Triplaris, are all for the reception of the protective ants. But we know that these structures have quite another meaning: the cavities in the base of Tillandsia are dried-up cisterns, the feltwork of aerial roots collects moisture and humus, the hollow stems of Triplaris serve to combine maximum elasticity with minimum material."

Where it can be shown that certain plants of which the leaf-cutters are fond have a bodyguard of ants, there is no reason to doubt that these are of protective advantage. This has been repeatedly proved by observation, especially in the case of some species of Cecropia (Imbauba or trumpet tree). These trees have smooth upright stems, raised on short aerial roots, and bearing simple branches, the whole appearance suggesting a gigantic candelabra. The leaves are few but very large. Now when one shakes a branch of the Cecropia, one rouses a wild army of ants, which with poisonous jaws resent the intrusion. Where do they all come from? Closer inspection shows little round apertures, especially on the upper internodes, which lead into the hollow stem.

In walking with the well-known naturalist Fritz Müller, Schimper saw a small Imbauba-tree which had been stripped of its leaves by the leaf-cutters. Fritz Müller ventured to affirm that in this case the bodyguard must have been absent, and in slicing up the stem he found not one. This was not an isolated case; the same has been repeatedly observed, so that we may safely conclude that a Cecropia tenanted by its bodyguard is relatively safe from the leaf-cutters.

The hollow stem with its horizontal partitions is plainly a comfortable home for the protective ants, but does it exhibit any structural peculiarities which must be referred to the insects? This cannot be said of the cavities themselves, but what of the doors? Each internode has at one time a door, which is obliterated by subsequent growth. The door is always in the same position; it is made by the ants at a spot where the wall of the stem thins away in an oval depression, and this is originally due to the pressure of a bud. There is no doubt that the beginning of the door arises quite apart from the ants, but on the other hand Schimper has detected a number of minute structural peculiarities connected with the door which he cannot explain except as adaptations to the visitors. On Cecropias which grow on the hill of Corcovado near Rio de Janeiro, and have very smooth wax-covered skins, ants are unrepresented, and the minute structure around the slight depression at which a door, were there one, would be formed, is quite different.

The ants find shelter within the Cecropia stem, but the tree also affords them abundant food. Near the base of the leaf-stalk there is on the under surface a small area covered with brown velvet-like hair, and on the surface of this are numerous pear-shaped or oval little bodies which look like insects' eggs. These ("Müller's bodies") are eaten by the ants, and they must be very nutritious, for their contents are rich in albuminoids and fatty oil. In their young stages they resemble the glands of other plants which secrete mucus or resin, and Francis Darwin has suggested that they are homologous with glands, but they are very peculiar, and their peculiarities Schimper would connect with the ants, for, strange to say, they are absent on Cecropias, such as those of Corcovado, on which there are no ants.

From Cecropia Schimper passes to other myrmecophilous plants, such as *Acacia sphærocephala*, whose hollow thorns afford shelter to a bodyguard, and which also bears little food-bodies comparable to those on Cecropia. But we have given sufficient illustration of this matter.

There is, however, another much-discussed subject on which Schimper has something interesting to tell us. We know that many of our flowers have honey-bags or nectaries, and that these are attractive lures to the bees and other insects which, in their search for sweets, carry the fertilising pollen from flower to flower. But often, especially in the Tropics, nectaries occur outside the flowers, as we have seen in Nepenthes.

Both Belt and Delpino regard these extra-floral nectaries as adaptations for the attraction of protective ants. Kerner supposes that they afford such generous supplies of nectaries that the ants leave the floral nectaries undisturbed; but this is not the way with ants! Bonnier regards them as stores of reserve-material; but the sugar is almost always stolen by ants or washed away by the rain. Johow has even suggested that they are receptacles for the waste-products formed in the movements of the leaves! but this too is for several reasons most unlikely, since it is enough to notice that they are especially large and numerous on the bracts which exhibit no movements.

Schimper concludes that the theory of Belt and Delpino is the only one which need be seriously considered. But before it can be believed that the extra-floral nectaries have arisen as adaptations to the protective ants, it must be shown, as Schimper rightly observes:—

(1) That the visits of the ants thus attracted afford so much protection, that without them the plant would be at a great disadvantage; and

(2) That the nectaries have not some other use in the economy of the plant, to which they are primarily referable.

By removing the extra-floral nectaries from various plants, Schimper has convinced himself that they are unnecessary and not demonstrably important for the wellbeing of the plant. They are most abundant where there are most ants. They certainly attract the ants, and these visitors sometimes, but by no means always ward off leaf-cutters. The plants which possess them may be worsted, but none the less they had an advantage as far as it went. In short, Schimper accepts the suggestion of Belt and Delpino. This conclusion has been further corroborated by W. Burck,[1] who finds that almost all plants with extra-floral nectaries or food-bodies are truly myrmecophilous, and proves by direct observation that the bodyguard of ants attracted by the nectaries are of important service in driving off marauding insects which spoil the foliage or perforate the corollas of the flowers without effecting fertilisation.

Domatia.—The homes which ants find inside the Acacia's thorns, or within the hollow stems of Cecropia, are not unique; Dr. Lundström has described under the title of *domatia* (meaning little homes) a large number of shelters on plants which are tenanted by harmless little

[1] *Ann. Jardin Bot. Buitenzorg*, x. (1891).

insects and mites. Sometimes they are like little wigwams formed from converging hairs, sometimes minute caves or pits. They are not formed by the tenants, at least not now, for they are natural to the plants, but they are none the less well adapted to the use they serve. A simple instance may be seen on the leaves of the lime-tree, on the under surface of which, at points where two veins of the leaf cross, there are little nooks tenanted by mites. These do not injure the plant, but rather help it, for they clear away minute fungi, and it is also possible that their nitrogenous waste-products are absorbed by the leaves.

Myrmecodia.—A pretty tale is that of *Myrmecodia tuberosa*, a rubiaceous plant from the Malayan Archipelago. The worthy Rumphius, still memorable as the pioneer naturalist of these regions, "describes it in his *Herbarium Amboynense* (1750) under the formidable but appropriate name of *Nidus germinans formicarum rubrarum*, and terms it "*prodigium naturæ*." He seems to have been uncertain whether the whole was a vegetable, or whether the tuber was an ant's nest from which the plant sprung; he says it is to be regarded as a zoophyte among vegetables! It presents the form of a large irregular tuber growing on the branches of old trees; from this spring a few thick fleshy stems, having a small number of smooth, leathery, oblong leaves crowded together at their summits. The small white sessile flowers are situated at the base of the petioles, and almost concealed by the large persistent stipules. The tuber is tenanted by small and very fierce red ants, which rush out upon the intruder if their dwelling is attacked. The way in which these ants take possession of the *Myrmecodia*, and the intimate relation which exists between the plant and the insect, are thus referred to in Professor Caruel's recent paper upon the genus.[1] The

[1] *Nuovo Giornale Botanico Italiano*, iv. pp. 170-176 (1872).

account is quoted from a manuscript note by Dr. Beccari who collected the plant in Borneo:—

"I have carefully followed the development of this tuber, having been able to observe the young plants in all stages of growth from the period of germination. The seed is surrounded by a viscid pulp, resembling that of our mistletoe, which readily attaches itself to the branches of the trees upon which it falls. Its dissemination is probably caused by means of the birds which eat the fruit, the undigested seed passing through them and adhering to the branches. The seed soon germinates and unfolds its cotyledons, especially if it has fallen in an opening of a branch where lichens have collected, or if it be placed in mould; the stem develops itself to the length of from three to six millimetres, widening towards the base, acquiring a somewhat conical shape, with the two cotyledons at its apex. In this condition it remains until a particular species of ant burrows a small lateral cavity at the base of the stem; if this does not happen, the stem does not develop itself, and the plant dies. The wound caused by the bite of the ant determines a great development of cellular tissue, in the same way as the sting of the cynips causes the galls on the oak. The tuber now enlarges and the stem develops; the ants soon find sufficient space for forming a colony, and excavate galleries in the interior of the tuber in all directions, thus making for themselves a living habitation—a circumstance which is necessary to the existence of the plant. The plant could not live or even arrive at maturity unless the ants contributed to the formation of the organ which must be the source from which it derives its support, while in all probability the ants could not exist or propagate themselves unless they had discovered this mode

quoted by Britten, "Ant-supporting Plants," *Popular Science Review.*

of constructing so ingenious a habitation. The fleshy substance of this formicarium is formed of cellular tissue; the channels and galleries with which it is perforated have their entrance near the lower part of the tuber."

Unluckily for Caruel and Beccari, the development of Myrmecodia has been reinvestigated lately by Treub,[1] in Java, who sadly diminishes the wonder by showing that the plant can thrive without its guests, and that the galleries are formed and grow as congenital peculiarities without the aid of ants. By rearing plants from the seed, in the absence of all ants, he has been able to study the growth of the tuberosities. They seem to him to be at first reservoirs in which water is stored for the needs of the plant, the firm outer surface (devoid of stomata or lenticels) preventing evaporation. The ants simply use these when dry as dwellings, without in any marked way benefiting the plant. This is a fresh lesson of caution, and of the risks of Darwinising over-much. A good specimen may be observed at Kew.

Galls. — These interesting domatia above referred to must of course be distinguished from the galls which many insects form on plants. Every one knows the large gall-nuts (rich in tannin and gallic acid, both useful in ink-making, etc.) formed on oak-leaves by wasp-like insects of the genus Cynips, and the strange "Bedeguar" tufts so common as mossy excrescences on wild roses. These abnormal growths are produced by a remarkable vegetative increase of the tissues of the plants. This is due to the irritation produced by the gall-flies, or rather gall-wasps, which lay their eggs in the soft substance of the plant. Here again, as with lichens or ants, or what not, we are but at the threshold of a new subject with its literature and its specialists. For along every main road of the organic

---

[1] "Nouvelles Recherches sur le Myrmecodia de Java," *Annales du Jardin Botanique de Buitenzorg*, vol. vii. (1888), p. 191.

sciences there branch off innumerable pleasant byways, each leading into a tiny world of its own, a minor infinity; at first sight no doubt a hazy labyrinth, yet on deepening study an ordered microcosm of evolutionary law.

Plants and Aphides. — From ants we naturally pass to the plant-lice or Aphides, for these little insects which form sweet juice receive much attention from the ants, who sometimes use them as cows.[1] Many of them, such as those which infest roses, fruit-trees, and hops, are exceedingly injurious to the plants, for they suck the sap, choke the pores of the leaves with their honey-dew, and do other damage. The honey-dew, of which the ants are so fond, has been for long the subject of much discussion. Pliny, and many later naturalists who should have known better, said that it fell from heaven; many have described it as an exudation from plants, while other — perhaps most — naturalists speak of two kinds — an animal honey-dew formed by the Aphides, and a vegetable honey-dew exuded in some way or other from the plants.

Büsgen's recent observations [2] lead him to affirm conclusively that all honey-dew, excepting sugary exudations caused by parasitic fungi, is an excretion of the Aphides. The only flow of sap from the cells of the plants is into the mouths of the insects; the sweet juices are slightly changed in the food-canal, but the quantity of glucose in this is out of proportion to the animal's wants, and hence what is unused as food passes out. As a single aphis may form as many as forty-eight drops of honey-dew in twenty-four hours, it is not surprising that a very rain of nectar should sometimes fall from trees (especially limes) which

[1] See conveniently J. Arthur Thomson, *The Study of Animal Life.* Lond. 1892.
[2] "Das Honig-Tau," *Jenaische Zeitschrift für Naturwissenschaft,* vol. xxv. (1891), pp. 339-428. 2 Pls.

are infested by thousands of these insects. Besides sapping the strength of the plant, and choking the leaves with honey-dew, the Aphides by their secretion make it easier for injurious parasitic fungi to establish themselves upon the leaves. On the other hand, they attract ants, whose presence in moderate numbers at any rate may be useful to the plants.[1] But as Herr Büsgen calculates that in one case the quantity of carbo-hydrate material absorbed by the Aphides from a plant was about one-sixth of that required to furnish the whole foliage, we must agree with him that this is too high a price to pay for problematical benefits.

The Ants and Aphides must serve as types of the injurious insects, between which and plants there are numerous interesting relations. We have to consider how far various structures of plants, such as hairy stems, viscid stems, pendent flowers, and the like, serve to save plants from their enemies, as may be true in the case of unwelcome ants; we have also to notice what changes the injurious insects, such as corn-insects, Phylloxera, Weevils, etc., may effect on the plants which they infest; and we must also observe how the hostile insects, which affect forest trees and vegetation generally, may occasion changes which have far-reaching influences on the fauna, flora, scenery, and even climate of a country-side. Readily available information will be found in Miss E. A. Ormerod's valuable work on *Injurious Insects* (second edition, Lond. 1891), while the more advanced student would do well to

---

[1] With all respect to this observer, one may still maintain that during prolonged fine weather, especially in June, while leaf tissues are fresh and young, and Aphides not yet abundant, such an excess of assimilation sometimes takes place as to create an overflow of nectar from leaves; the very ferns sometimes showing this without Aphides upon them, or at any rate in adequate numbers.

consult the researches of Riley, Packard, and others in the Bulletins of the United States Entomological Commission, from which many detailed illustrations of the web of life may be gleaned.

Cats and Clover.—We have only given a few illustrations of the infinite number of interactions between plants and animals; other examples and of more importance, *e.g.* in connection with the fertilisation of the flowers and the scattering of seeds, will be referred to again. As with insectivorous or moving plants, the writer's aim is to familiarise the reader with the essential point of view at which Darwin has placed us,—his appreciation of the dramatic complexity of nature; as also of the task of the least. Nature is no longer a mere confused multitude of specimens to be collected and analysed, but each organism is linked with others as consecutively as in the "House that Jack Built"; nay, with indefinite cross relations as well: what seemed a unit is a link; what seemed a chain is but a thread within the labyrinthine web of nature. That in thus opening out for us this new and fascinating study of bionomics, he has exaggerated the importance of the selective factor in evolution, and that the drama is not merely of incident and adventure but of *character* also, is a secondary consideration, though an important one; since but for Darwin we might hardly yet have realised that there is an organic drama at all.

He takes a ball of mud from off the leg of a bird, and finds that out of it no less than eighty seeds germinate! He shows how cattle absolutely determine the existence of the Scotch fir on the Surrey heath, or how insects determine the absence of wild cattle and horses in Paraguay. "If certain insectivorous birds were to decrease in Paraguay, the parasitic insects would probably increase; and this would lessen the number of flies which destroy the young horses and cattle—then the latter would become feral, and this would certainly greatly alter the vegetation; this again would largely affect the insects; and this the insectivorous birds, and so onwards in ever-increasing circles of complexity." So, too, with the terrible tsetse fly, which, as Livingstone pointed out, renders pasturage and animal transport impossible within its region, so condemning civilisation to a lower type.

But perhaps his best illustration is the most familiar one, which should never become trite to us. "Plants and animals, remote in the scale of nature, are bound together by a web of complex relations. . . . I have found from experiments that humble-bees are almost indispensable to the fertilisation of the heartsease (*Viola tricolor*), for other bees do not visit this flower. I have also found that the visits of bees are necessary for the fertilisation of some kinds of clover—thus, 100 heads of red clover (*Trifolium pratense*) produced 27,000 seeds, but the same number of protected heads produced not a single seed. Humble-bees alone visit red clover, as other bees cannot reach the nectar. . . . Hence we may infer as highly probable that, if the whole genus of humble-bees became extinct or very rare in England, the heartsease and red clover would become very rare, or wholly disappear. The number of humble-bees in any district depends in a great measure on the number of field-mice, which destroy their combs and nests; and Colonel Newman, who has long attended to the habits of humble-bees, believes that more than two-thirds of them are thus destroyed all over England."[1] Now the number of mice is largely dependent, as every one knows, on the number of cats; and Colonel Newman says, "Near villages and small towns I have found the nests of humble-bees more numerous than elsewhere, which I attribute to

[1] *Origin of Species*, chap. iii. Lond. 1859.

the number of cats that destroy the mice." Hence it is quite credible that the presence of a feline animal in large numbers in a district might determine, through the intervention first of mice and then of bees, the frequency of certain flowers in that district.

This may seem a mere matter for naturalists, yet in this connection we touch on practical politics. The British farmer is at this day in many districts sorely exercised by a plague of field-mice and voles with which sheep-pastures are notably swarming. How far is this due to the relentless war waged by the gamekeeper against owls, ferrets, weasels, and all the other mouse-loving creatures, furry or feathered? The Board of Agriculture in the person of Mr. Chaplin, decides not, suggesting climatic causes as the explanation of the pests, if not almost hinting at occult ones, beyond the penetration of human intelligence.[1] But on what grounds, *i.e.* on what actual observation and investigation does this deliverance rest? If none, might not the Board of Agriculture as profitably encourage it to be made by the farmers and field-naturalists of each district? The result could not but be instructive; perhaps unexpected.[2]

[1] It is of course not inconceivable that we may have in animals as in trees, good "seed-years"; *i.e.* some internal rhythm larger than the annual one, of unusual fecundity.

[2] As this goes to press, I am glad to learn that the step has been taken of forming a committee to investigate the questions.

CHAPTER VIII

SPRING AND ITS STUDIES; GEOGRAPHICAL DISTRIBUTION
AND WORLD-LANDSCAPES; SEEDLING AND BUD

Spring Studies — Mode of Study in Botany — Phenology and Distribution — Aspects of Nature, Vegetation and Landscapes of the World — Germination — Buds and Bud-Scales — Arrangement of Leaves in the Bud.

THE study of plants is naturally begun in spring. It is, indeed, the supreme advantage of a temperate climate, — one which richly compensates in beauty and even in interest for a verdure less exuberant, a variety less Protean than that of the tropical forest, — that the procession of the seasons is ever before us. Life is, indeed, universally rhythmic, in animal as in plant; but the plant is more passive and plastic to its conditions, more under the sway of environmental change, and hence this seasonal change of plant life becomes the more impressive spectacle of living nature. See the tide of life set in with a flood in spring, filling every corner of the earth with sprouting seeds and shooting stems, and crowding, spreading, rippling leaves; how as the russet underwood warms to the fuller sun through trees still bare, it glows with bright golden patches of lesser celandine; how its dead leaves silently sink under a restless foam-tipped sea of green anemone; how every mossy bank is set with primroses in crowded constellation; and how the deep summer sky shows first in sheets of hyacinth. Soon comes high tide of leaves in June: the full-robed year is crowned and garlanded with exuberant blossom, to which July brings the strongest chords of colour. Yet already the tide has turned, the flowers are withering or fading, but a new profusion of fruits, more strangely varied even than the flowers, is rising in their place. These, too, ripen and pass, and the seeds, each a young life, find, ofttimes through strange adventure, their resting-place and sleep. The shivering leaves surrender their life to the branches which have borne them, and fall away, often strangely transfigured in dying; only their tiny nurslings the buds remain, warmly wrapped away within their protecting sheaths. Life has ebbed out of sight; Proserpina is in Hades, and sky and mother earth must mourn till her release.

Mode of Study in Botany. — Here then is the common theme not only of poets old and new, of painters, but of naturalists. Each, indeed, has his own way of treating this; and each way involves its special difficulties, its risks of error. For the poet and the painter the detailed exactitude are of subordinate importance, hence both have often fallen into mere echoes and conventions: the town poet in parrot whine of Proserpine without one true glimpse of her yearly Paradise or Hades; the painter (as if confined to the latter) with his "brown tree." For the botanist the danger has been a different one. As his herborisations have needs become keener and of more minute research, his herbarium labours more vast and detailed, his laboratory and microscope more engrossing and their new problems more intricate, his library, too, more incredibly voluminous, even his greenhouses better filled, his real intimacy with living nature as a whole has often diminished rather than increased; until he writes manuals and treatises excellent often as grammars, and in any case copious as dictionaries, of the science; yet with these most general of all phenomena under consideration, left unmentioned in the one, nay, the very technical name of their study — *Phenology* — alone forgotten in the crowded columns of the other. Whereas here is the essential "course" in the subject indicated — say rather openly revealed — to student and teacher by Nature herself with clearness as in no other science. For the child then, *Flora's Feast* is as yet the best, almost the only true primer of botany; for the older student the *Natural History of Selborne* remains a central and inspiring classic. The more developed and systematised *Naturalist's Diary* is the best *vade mecum*, to which a Flora (perferably a district or county one) comes in as a subordinate, though indispensable adjunct, and desirably also any simple manual of garden flowers. "Am I to read no text-books then?" the dismayed student constantly asks. The writer for one answers, with deeper and better justified conviction every year, Read? certainly not; Consult? yes, constantly, by help of the index, for every point and difficulty as it arises, for all information as it is desired. Thus you will gradually get all the facts and results and methods which it contains, while thus, and probably thus only, can you avoid that elaborately formalist analysis of the subject from which every science has such difficulty to escape. Botany is a drama of nature, and this summer is your opportunity of seeing it. That text-book is not really a book of the play; of that we have as yet only a multifarious and scattered polyglot literature, the jottings and notes of many hands; and though the text-book is for practical purposes your first guide to the literature, — it may be almost your only substitute for it, — you must bear in mind that its careful summaries of results of research are but new patches upon an old garment, new wine in old bottles. That is to say, that however useful and truly botanical its matter, the arrangement and presentment of your text-book is not that of either botanist or nature at all, but is directly and historically (however unconsciously) derived from that traditional discipline of grammar and analysis which in the name of literature have been crushing out the love of literature, even the knowledge of literature, in every university and school of Europe for centuries, and from which we are now only beginning to escape. Its list of *dramatis personæ* will be constantly useful for reference; its dictionary may help from time to time as well; its grammar of the science may be discussed later. Let the evolutionary way of looking at things become gradually familiar, then habitual, at last instinctive; then you may profitably consider the best way of arrangement of your ideas — in fact, make your scientific grammar for yourself. But this will be in sharpest contrast to the old one, no longer fixed or static, but historical, kinetic; rational therefore, not merely empirical, synthetic instead of analytic in spirit and result. And when you endeavour to make the unending stream of things intelligible by the artifice of viewing it in section as it were, as momentarily frozen and photographed at this or that point upon its course, you will sympathetically interpret and profitably absorb the pre-evolutionary method, which has, of course, been doing this all the while. In plainer language, instead of being (as the established programmes have it) an anatomist first, dissecting a dead "type," a physiologist afterwards making its parts work, and an evolutionist by getting up Darwin's theory as an external body of dogma last of all, the right course is precisely the opposite: Darwin's habit of observation and interpretation first, physiological details afterwards, with such anatomy as is wanted to explain them. Thereafter, of course, such pure morphology as you will.

Phenology and Distribution. — Returning from the manner to the matter of our studies, let us look more fully at this most general aspect of the science — its "phenologcial" and geographical side. Astronomers have long ago connected the waxing and waning of the redness of Mars with the seasonal changes of its year; and some suggest that this change of colour may be explained not merely as that of soil more or less exposed by the varying area of polar snow-caps, but as connected with the annual changes of a *red* vegetation, or what may answer to vegetation. However this may be, if we imagine an astronomer observing our earth from Mars, or of course more conveniently from the nearer standpoint of the moon, he could not fail to be impressed by the waxing and waning of her verdant belt. And if we imagine him granted what he would wish — the means of viewing this strange phenomenon more clearly and in detail — he becomes a botanical geographer.

The botanist thus begins his studies where the astronomer ends, and travels over the whole earth with the geographer; he is no mere student of detail gathering specimens to catalogue or anatomise, but, like each of these, holds the globe between his hands; nay, takes it from them not only for a keener survey, but for a clearer, richer, and fuller one, landscape by landscape. He is, in fact, twin brother to the landscape-painter; and while at one moment absorbed like a pre-Raphaelite draughtsman amid the fascinating wealth of foreground detail, is at the next an impressionist melting down this detail into the richer tone and broader colour of a larger truth.

Hence then, although we have entered the botanical school by way of its greenhouse and collection, and looked into its laboratories of physiology and histology, we are only now reaching the larger aspect of the science. How shall we proceed to deepen our acquaintance with this? Although, as in every study, difficulties are not lacking, the student may here start from common experience and with advantages common to few sciences — those of observation in his holiday walk and study in his general reading.

"Aspects of Nature," Vegetation and Landscapes of the World. — Let him search out in the nearest library a famous yet too much forgotten book, Humboldt's *Cosmos*, or at any rate run through his *Aspects of Nature* with its passages of imperishable description; let him turn over the stately folios of botany and travel in an old library, and look over the plates of Martius's *Palms* and the like. Let him read Darwin's *Naturalist's Voyage*, Wallace's *Malay Archipelago*, his *Tropical Nature*, and *Island Life*; gleaning too the descriptive passages of books of travel, even by non-botanists, so gaining detail from one book and colour from another until he has some general idea of the vegetation of the world so far as his accessible library resources go. The plates of, say, the *Botany* of the Challenger Expedition will thus get colour from the glowing prose pictures of Kingsley's dying voyage: Stanley's dark forest, Ruskin's alpine flower-meadow and lichened rocks, Wordsworth's daffodils — all will help to fill this gallery of the imagination. But why should this gallery be in the imagination only? To make these thought representations science, they must be permanent and precise, ordered and complete. Here begins the interest of the collections of a botanic garden, especially where geographically arranged, as partly at Kew, or notably at Berlin. Yet to make all this more real and vivid, we need pictures. For

> We're made so that we love
> First when we see them painted, things we have passed
> Perhaps a hundred times nor cared to see;
> And so they are better, painted — better to us,

> Which is the same thing. Art was given for that;
> God uses us to help each other so,
> Lending our minds out.

Here Miss North's collection at Kew is of special interest;[1] and although the botanist is apt to turn away disappointed with the lack of arrangement of this wealth of sketches, and the artist with their pictorial quality, both will admit at least that here is a beginning full of suggestiveness: and if so, why should not both go to work together, — student working for artist, and artist for student, — until a permanent gallery of landscapes and vegetation is the result; an ever-widening panorama, by help of which we may vividly realise what the world is like?

But we cannot all travel like Miss North, it may be said. Still, make the best of it; look at our familiar walks like geographical botanists, even within a couple of hours' walk of a great manufacturing town, and behold, each little scene stretches itself out over the world-map as if by enchantment. Shall we stroll along the sand-dunes blue with the waving of their binding-reed? What we see is half the eastern shore of our whole island, and well-nigh the whole western coast of the Low Countries opposite, whence we may wander with the sea-birds along the whole length of Prussia, and over to Sweden, or up to the Gulf of Bothnia. Or to the cliffs, with their bright tufts of sea-pink and bladderwort, their close-set turfy slopes? This is the coast of Brittany and Norway; and these two pictures will well-nigh frame for us the whole North Sea. Or shall we sketch these stretches of unreclaimed moorland, here golden with whin or purple with heather, and there with dwarfish willows rising above an undergrowth of grass and sedges,

---

[1] See the Kew Catalogue of North Collection by Mr. W. B. Hemsley, and *Recollections of a Happy Life, being the Autobiography of Marianne North.* 2 vols. London, 1892.

with patches of turf-moss, their chilly gray lightened only by the silver pillar of a struggling birch? If so, this bit of moorland is a surviving fragment of the great heath of northern Europe, through which every one who enters Germany from Rotterdam or Hamburg must still run for so many weary miles, and of which the vast area of cultivation up to the Ural may be almost described as an imperfect clearing. East of the Ural the bogs and peat-mosses widen, the heaths leave us, the willows and birches remain — it is the gray tundra of North Siberia. So our afternoon's stroll, with its couple of sketches, gives the essential general impression of five thousand miles.

Nor are these surviving fragments of natural landscapes the only ones; there are good artificial landscapes as well. Would we roam through the deciduous forest scenery of the lower Alps? The neglected corners of that old park are not to be despised. Or the sombre pine-woods of Sweden? That little loch among the hills, its shores close planted to the very margin, will fairly serve. Or would we see rhododendrons of America or Asia, the quaint conifers of California, the evergreens of Japan or of the Mediterranean? They are in every shrubbery. Do we seek the richer vegetation of the warm temperate zone, the ferny wealth of the antipodes, the stately leafage of a tropical forest? That greenhouse, that botanic garden palmhouse, shows us these in some ways at their very best. So too we shall come better to understand the gardener in his highest capacity as offering us the resources of an art vaster and grander than that of cities.

For this geographical botany we need now only more precise scientific guidance. The article DISTRIBUTION of Chambers's *Encyclopædia* may serve as a starting point; then the appropriate chapter of any good manual of physical geography, conveniently Mill's *Realm of Nature* in this series;

best of all of course Drude's *Pflanzenverbreitung* and his section of Berghaus's great Physical Atlas, which is happily soon to be available in improved form for English readers.

The student thus equipped, and the artist practised in rendering these scenes in colour, they may now with safety avail themselves of the help of books and photographs in extending their collection of paintings; friendly criticism can often be obtained from travellers who actually have visited these scenes, and a growing collection of no little interest and value to more than the pure botanist be thus gradually obtained. Why should not any knot of friends, of whom some love painting and others botany, work together in this way? There is plenty of blank wall space in the nearest school to hang their labours with endless pleasure and usefulness to children, teachers, and naturalists alike.[1] Nor is such a collection unworthy the attention of the conservators of museums and art galleries, and of the geographical societies.

Germination. — One of the many wise sayings of Erasmus Darwin was, that the offspring of any organism was not so much a new creature as "a branch or elongation of the parent." This is the common characteristic of all kinds of reproduction, whether of plants or of animals, that part of the parent is separated off to begin a new life. In most cases the new life begins from the union of two units, pro-

---

[1] The writer has here to express his thanks to the Dundee Art Club, whose members have gone far with the preparation of such a collection of paintings for the botanical department of the College; to Mr. Maclauchlan, curator of the City Museum Library and Art Gallery, for much help; as also to the studio of the Edinburgh Summer Meeting. With his friend and former pupil, Miss Etta Johnston, whose share in this matter has been a very active one, he will be happy to give all information and assistance to others who may wish to begin such a collection.

duced by two parent organisms, but the separated parts or units are in a very deep way continuations of the life of the parents, formed of the same living material as that which gave origin to the parents, able therefore when separated to grow into similar organisms.

When we examine seeds, such as those of beans or peas, we at once see that they are not simple structures like, for instance, the eggs of birds. It is easy to convince ourselves that each ripe seed already contains a young plant, with a little stem and root, and in the cases above mentioned, with two seed-leaves or cotyledons packed full of what we know to be nutritious matter. Seeds are not comparable to the eggs but to the embryos of animals. To find out what corresponds to the egg we must examine under the microscope thin slices of unripe seeds or ovules, in the midst of which we may be able to see a small unit — known as the egg-cell. This it is which, after being fertilised by a pollen-grain, develops into an embryo plant within the seed. A seed is in fact the most complex and long-discarded marvel within the field of botany, of which the full unravelment and interpretation lies beyond the compass of the present volume. In accordance with the bionomic or Darwinian principle of study here advocated, the student may be advised first to study its more obvious and external history of dispersal and of adaptation by help of some such interesting and convenient volume as Sir John Lubbock's *Flowers, Fruits, and Leaves*, or Kerner's *Pflanzenleben*, Leipzig, 2 vols., already mentioned: the latter being by far the richest store of information accessible to the general reader, and, thanks to its wealth of illustration both coloured and in the text, of great use and interest even where there is no knowledge of German; after this, the minute anatomy of the seed, with the comprehension of its morphological secret, and the evolutionary meaning of this will be all the better appreciated.

In the great majority of cases the embryo plant is fully formed by the time the seeds are scattered in autumn. Let us see what happens to the seed after it falls into the ground.

Every one has heard stories of "mummy wheat," which after lying for many centuries in the tombs was still alive, and germinated when sown; or of the raspberry grown from seed gathered among the ribs of a Roman soldier. Although these stories are not justified by sufficiently careful experiment, they express, in exaggeration, a fact characteristic of most seeds, that in natural conditions they remain for a time quiescent before they begin to germinate. Throughout the winter their life is dormant, and if conditions do not change — as notably through depth of burial — the dormant period may be lengthened in a degree varying with the species, and not yet sufficiently determined by experiment, but certainly often extending to many years.

This period of quiescence depends, however, only in part upon external conditions, such as the depth or the frost-bound hardness of the soil; in part, too, upon the husks which protect and imprison the embryo plant, and must be softened before it can burst forth; but also on internal processes of fermentation, as the result of which the supply of food becomes changed into more available form. In fact, the process of digestion, which we recognised as an apparently extraordinary thing in insectivorous plants, occurs normally in the life of seeds. The stores of organic substances — which make seeds important parts of our food — are rendered soluble and diffusible before and during germination. There is not only a diastatic ferment which converts starchy material into sugar, but there are others, such as that which Professor J. R. Green has so carefully studied in the seeds of Lupin — a ferment which acts like the pancreatic juice of animals, converting the proteids of the seed into diffusible peptones, and then into leucin, asparagin, etc., quite as in the animal process.

The spring showers water the earth, the moisture softens the husks of the seeds, and soaking inwards recalls the living matter to activity; the ferments which we have mentioned convert the stores of food into a form available for transport and use; the temperature of the earth is slightly raised, so helping the reawakening. Soon, as we know, the radicle pushes its way out of the seed and into the soil, the tiny stem arches its way above the ground, on this the tender leaves (sometimes first the cotyledons) spread forth. By all means watch how the germination of the grain of wheat differs from that of the pea, and the mustard seedling from that of the cedar; meantime we are concerned only with the general fact.

By means of a simple experiment we can get a hint of the intensity of life in germinating seeds. Take a glass vessel and put into it a small quantity of caustic potash; into the mouth of the vessel place a glass funnel, and after inserting a piece of filter paper, fill the funnel with moist germinating seeds, such as those of wheat or peas; cover the whole with a bell-jar, through the corked neck of which a thermometer descends into the midst of the seeds. As the cork is not air-tight, air enters the jar freely enough, and the caustic potash absorbs the carbonic acid gas formed by the living and breathing seeds. As these go on germinating, the thermometer registers a marked increase of temperature. Breathing and living imply oxidation of some of the complex substances of the seeds, and, as in ordinary combustion, the oxidation is associated with the liberation of heat. In making this experiment it is well to make at the same time a duplicate of it with this difference only, that boiled peas or the like are substituted for the germinating ones; in this case it is hardly necessary to say the thermometer indicates no change. But what is true of the living seeds would for a short time be true also of flower-heads or of opening buds.

Buds. — We have spoken of seedlings as characteristic of spring, and to a certain extent this may be said of buds also. The bud is to the branch on which it grows what the seed is to the entire plant. And just as most seeds in temperate countries are formed during summer, are scattered in autumn, lie dormant throughout the winter, and begin to grow in spring, so most buds are well formed by autumn, remain quiescent within their protective scales during winter, and burst forth in spring into twigs and leaves. It is this unfolding of the bud which is characteristic of spring-time.

But let us seek to gain a more precise conception of what a bud is. Every one is familiar with the appearance of a split cabbage: in the centre there is a portion of stem tapering to its growing point; around this, springing from different levels, are many layers of crowded crumpled leaves covering the growing point in overlapping layer after layer. Now a cabbage is an exaggerated bud, or, to put it in another way, every bud is a sort of incipient cabbage.

Going back to the seed, we find in the plumule and the minute leaves which often lie around its tip, the primeval bud, a rudiment of the stem and its appendages. We see the same thing at a later stage in the growing point of the stem; there is a central continuation of the axis, and around this are several tiers, or rather spirals — in technical language, *whorls* — of young leaves.

Very frequently among Monocotyledons (plants like grasses, lilies, and orchids) the bud which forms the apex of the stem alone develops, and thus we have the unbranched stems of palms (fig. 7). But in most Dicotyledons (the majority of flowering plants) the numerous buds, which

Fig. 7. — Assai palm (*Euterpe oleracia*). (After Bates.)

are usually situated in the axils of leaves, develop and shoot forth as leaf-bearing branches or as flowers.

In our common trees, and indeed in most of the perennial plants of temperate climates, the buds are well formed in autumn. For a time there is active growth, but this is checked by the advent of winter, during which the buds remain dormant. When the frost is unusually keen the tender life of the bud is sometimes killed, but this is usually obviated by the protective scales with which the bud is enclosed. Just as the outer older leaves of the cabbage envelop the inner leaves, so is it in the bud. But there is more than this; the outer parts are modified — by an arrest of development, or even partial dying — into firm scales, which are often waterproofed with an exudation of resinous varnish, or warmly lined with epidermic down. Moreover, the inner leaves of the bud are kept close together, bent over the growing point of the stem, for it seems that at first their under surfaces grow more rapidly than the upper surfaces — the very reverse of what afterwards takes place when the buds burst and the leaves unfold.

Bud-Scales. — If we look at a number of buds we see various arrangements which secure their better protection against the cold of winter. In the simplest cases, *e.g.* lilac and rhododendron, the bud-scales are modifications of entire leaves: in fact, in a notably exceptional case among our deciduous trees, that of the Wayfaring tree (*Viburnum Lantana*), the lowest leaves serve as bud-scales — that is, the bud-scales, thanks to their woolly coating, are able to survive and develop as ordinary foliage leaves. In other cases, they correspond simply to the broadened stalks of leaves, and if we examine branches of the horse-chestnut or walnut in spring we shall find occasional examples of every stage between the foliage-leaf with its five leaflets and the usual reduced bud-scale. Finally, bud-scales may be derived, as in the beech, from those little appendages of leaves which we call stipules. When spring comes, and the bud passes from a latent to an active period, the protective scales — often almost dead — are thrown off, and often carpet and tint the ground like a foreshadowing of autumn. The autumn indeed it is for these sacrificed leaves which are to know no summer.

Arrangement of the Leaves in the Bud (Phyllotaxis). — It is interesting to dissect a few buds to see the various ways in which the young leaves are packed together, a great number being compressed into the small space. This neat packing has the further importance that it mainly determines the position of the leaves on the future stem or branch. We have all observed the regular arrangement of scales in a fir-cone or of leaves in a crowded rosette like that of a house-leek, stiff and orderly as in a prize double camellia, but so it is really in the longest stem. Mark the knots upon a thorn walking-stick; see the house-leek send up its long scanty-leaved flower-stalk; imagine the fir-cone pulled out; or reverse the experiment, and let a stretched elastic cord stand for a stem; wind round this, in ascendings spirals at regular distances, a string bearing knots to represent leaf insertions, or still better, holding paper leaves or real ones, also of course at regular distances. Then allow the elastic cord to contract; the leaves will bend to assume positions such as occurs in nature within a bud. Twist the cord, and the leaf-spiral becomes more crowded and complex, the leaves therefore more perfectly packed one upon another; so we may reproduce the spirals of different plants. Here then, especially if of any mathematical tastes, we have an interesting field of inquiry — What are the different spirals to be met with in plants? how far are these constant or related? what effect will an abnormality such as the fusion of two scales in a fir-cone have upon the spirals? and so on. Much new light upon morphology used to be hoped for from this study, notably by Alexander Braun of Berlin, half a century ago; and in our own day the late Professor Dickson has been its most elegant and subtle expositor,[1] as Schwendener its most productive student; it has, however, for most botanists a diminished interest, although we may still hope it holds some floral secrets.

More important, however, from our present point of view, is the use of this spiral. For most botanists this used to be explained simply as keeping each leaf out of the light of its predecessor (or out of the shadow of its successor, if we prefer to put it so); Airy, however, in an interesting paper suggested by Darwin, inclines to interpret it primarily as an adaptation to more perfect bud-packing, as bove indicated. Its deeper explanation of course lies in some spiral growth-rhythm which we do not as yet clearly understand.

From seeds and their germination, from buds and their unfolding, we naturally pass to the life of the adult plant. How is that life sustained from day to day? The seed had a store of food within itself, and the growth of the young plant is for a time comparable to that of the embryo chick within the egg. The store of food within the grain of wheat is analogous to the yolk of the egg. But after that is exhausted, how is life sustained? We have already seen that a plant — in some ways so like a sleeping animal — often wakes up in movement, and although the movements are not often so conspicuous as in the climbers, the facts that plants do always move a little, that they force their way into the ground and raise themselves into the air, that, in

[1] The student may with advantage read his chapter on Phyllotaxis in Balfour's *Elements of Botany*.

short, they live and grow, should be enough to convince us that they must feed in some way, no less than animals. In our study of insectivorous plants we saw some strange examples of feeding, and in chap. iv., in considering the plant not as an isolated thing, but as part of the great system of nature, we got glimpses of some of the ordinary relations of plants to the air, to the soil, and to radiant energy. Let us seek to get a more precise conception of these relations, let us see how the important parts of a plant — leaves, roots, and stem — are adapted to the sustenance of the life. Let us look closely at these different parts, and see how their forms are suited to, and modelled partly by, the uses which they have to perform, partly by the surrounding conditions in which they live: in technical language, let us consider the adaptation of plant-structure to function and environment. For this we can have no better type than is given by a fuller study of the leaf, to which we may therefore turn.

CHAPTER IX

LEAVES

General Facts in Regard to the Life of Leaves — Experiments, Rough and Exact — Summary of Leaf Functions — The Structure of the Leaf — Palisade Cells and Chlorophyll Grains — Shapes of Leaves — Leaves adapted to Special Functions — Substitutes for Leaves — Vitality of the Leaf — Fall of the Leaf.

General Facts in Regard to the Life of Leaves. — The leaf is the most distinctive part of the plant. There are many rootless plants, such as the bladderwort which we have already described; there are many plants without stems, such as the seaweeds; but few plants can be called leafless. Where the leaves are suppressed the stem is modified to take their place.

The leaf may be also viewed as the primitive part of the plant. For among the seaweeds there is nothing but leaf, there are no true stems nor roots. The liverworts, which spread over the damp banks of streams, are still mostly leaf, provided, however, with suctorial rootlets on their under surfaces. With the mosses and the ferns stems begin.

It is therefore natural to suppose that the leaf is the most essential part of the plant so far as the sustenance of life is concerned. We shall see how true this is. Let us think over the familiar facts in regard to the life of plants which may give us hints as to the nature of the leaf.

First then in spring the bursting of the buds and the unfolding of the leaves to the lengthening day; then how at the approach of winter, when the conditions of light, heat, and moisture are no longer favourable, the leaves fall off, and there is no obvious growth after they are gone. Note too the many differences between the fresh growing leaves and those which have withered and fallen off; for one thing, the former are rich in starch and sugar, and other substances which the dead leaves lack. In dying at any rate the leaves surrender the best of their substance to the permanent body of the plant. We shall see that they are doing this all their life long.

When voracious insects eat up all the leaves of a plant and leave it bare, death often follows, although stem and root are quite uninjured. And when a plant has received some shock, as of frost or heat or poisonous smoke, or is scarce of water, one of the first symptoms of ill-health — often a very rapid symptom — is the drooping of the leaves, so essential are they to the sustained life of the plant.

Again, we are all familiar with the eatableness of many leaves, such as those of cabbage, spinach, and lettuce; they are swollen out in great part with water, but also with nutritive materials; so we get an idea of the leaf as a part of the plant in which substances are manufactured and sometimes stored up.

Experiments in Regard to Leaves. — More precise ideas about the uses of leaves may be gained by a few simple experiments. Let us follow one of these described by Detmer.

Take some seeds, such as those of wheat, maize, and beans; weigh them, and let them germinate and grow in water to which some plant ashes have been added. But in order to get a more precise measurement of the amount of material with which you begin, take samples of the seeds used, grind them to powder, thoroughly dry them at a high temperature, and weigh them. In this way the proportion of water in the seeds may be estimated, and by simple calculation it is easy to make an approximate statement as to the amount of solid, and for the most part organic, matter in the seeds used for the experiment. By and by, in favourable conditions of light and heat, the plants (let us say of maize) grow up and bear leaves. Let them flourish for several weeks, and then remove them from the vessel in which they have been growing; dry off superficial moisture, cut them into small pieces, and thoroughly dry a fair sample of these at a high temperature sufficient to drive off the internal water. It is thus easy to estimate how much new organic matter the plant has made for itself during these weeks. We say organic matter (starch and the like), because the proportion of inorganic matter, estimated by weighing the ash left after the whole is burned, is very small, and may for the present be left out of account. Now the experiment shows that in the course of its growth the plant has gained greatly in organic matter. Where has that come from? Partly, no doubt, from the water and salts; but that can be measured, and does not account for the total increase of weight, nor do the water and salts account at all for the carbon, which is the essential element in all organic compounds. The answer to our question every one knows; the plant has absorbed carbonic acid gas from the air, and has built the carbon thus obtained along with the elements of water, and in part also with the elements of salts, into complex organic substances. But by what means was the carbonic acid gas absorbed from the air? If we look at our maize plant there can hardly be but one answer—by means of the leaves. But if one of the vessels containing germinated maize is placed in darkness and allowed to grow there for some time, the resulting plants, which are lean and blanched, actually weigh less (when dried) than the seeds did. Instead of a gain in organic matter, there has been a loss, due to the living and breathing of the plant. In other words, in the absence of light the plant is not green, and is unable to utilise the carbonic acid gas of the air. So we may say of the leaves that they are those green parts by means of which the plant is in sunlight able to utilise the carbonic acid gas of the air and to build up organic substances.

Another experiment of profound importance is readily made. Take a piece of some vigorous water-plant, such as the Canadian pondweed *Elodea* (*Anacharis*) *canadensis*, so common in streams and canals; place it in a vessel of water into which some carbonic acid gas (easily produced in a separate vessel by decomposing carbonate of lime with hydrochloric acid) may with advantage have been introduced. Place the vessel with the pondweed in the sunlight, and watch the little bubbles of gas which appear on the leaves and ascend to the surface. Place a funnel over the plant, and catch the bubbles of gas in a test-tube filled with water and inverted over the tube of the funnel. Gradually as the bubbles ascend into the test-tube they displace the water, and if you have patience you will at last have the test-tube full of the gas. If you carefully remove the test-tube and push into it a smouldering match, it will glow brightly and perhaps catch fire again, or in other less rough-and-ready ways you can show that the gas in the tube is very rich in oxygen. The leaves, therefore are organs which in sunlight give off oxygen, this being another aspect of their power of utilising the carbonic acid gas. The oxygen which they liberate results from the breaking up of the molecules of carbonic acid gas within the plant.

That the Canadian pondweed absorbs, like other water-plants, its requisite supply of carbonic acid gas from what is dissolved in the water, while most plants absorb it from the mixture of gases in the atmosphere, is an unimportant detail. These experiments can be readily varied and extended; thus we might put roots in place of the leaves in our last experiment, but no bubbles of oxygen would be formed; or we might place the pondweed in water from which the carbonic acid had been expelled by boiling, and allow no air to enter the vessel except through a tube of caustic potash, which will absorb its carbonic acid, with the result that the evolution of oxygen would entirely cease.

More Exact Experiment. — A rough analysis of the evolved gases can easily be made by collecting them in a graduated tube, shaking up first with potash solution to absorb all traces of carbonic acid, and then adding pyrogallic acid, which absorbs the oxygen and leaves only the nitrogen (with a little water-vapour). This method becomes of the greatest ease, rapidity, and exactitude, as also delicacy in dealing with the smallest quantities of gases by help of the apparatus recently introduced by MM. Bonnier and Mangin (*Revue Générale de Botanique* 1890), which is figured below. It will be found of great use to the teacher of practical botany, as also to the experimentalist, especially in our uncertain climate.

Experiment can show us many other things about leaves. It is commonly known that a starch solution turns a deep blue colour when a little iodine solution is added to it. We may use this fact, as Sachs recommends, to demonstrate the presence of starch in leaves. If some leaves, *e.g.* of sunflower or of potato, are placed for a few minutes in boiling water, and then for a short time in warm alcohol, they become colourless. The green colouring matter or chlorophyll is dissolved by the alcohol. If the discoloured leaves are then placed for an hour or two in the dilute alcoholic solution of iodine, and then removed to a saucer full of water, those which were rich in starch assume the characteristic blue colour. Of this test for starch we can make many other uses; by growing plants in darkness, or in an atmosphere without any carbonic acid gas, we can show that starch is not formed in the leaves unless they are green, unless they are illumined, unless they are growing in a medium where carbonic acid gas is available.

The leaves are able to manufacture many other organic substances besides starch, and their presence is also of course demonstrable by experiment, but starch is com-

FIG. 8.—Apparatus of Bonnier and Mangin, for analysis of gases given off by plants. c, *Reservoir of Mercury;* m m, graduated tube; v, screw of piston, which enables the gas to be drawn into the graduated tube and measured; and after it the potash and pyrogallic solutions successively each being thoroughly brought into contact with the gas in the dilatations a.

monest and simplest, and may well serve as a type of the products built up by the life of the leaf.

It is also very important to show by experiment, by the analysis of plant ashes, and by growing seeds in artificially-prepared solutions, that certain salts, especially nitrates and sulphates, are essential to the health of the plant and to the leaf's manufacture of complex organic substances. The successive omission of each particular ingredient gives rise to some recognisable defect of growth, *e.g.* when iron is absent we have a blanched plant, while verdure returns on the addition of a drop of ferric chloride. It is also possible to prepare culture solutions in which all necessary constituents are present, and thus to grow many plants without soil. In many leaves it is easy to demonstrate the presence of oxalate of lime — we can taste it in the wood-sorrel and the sour-dock — and this salt seems to be a by-product of chemical reactions which go on in the leaf in which the nitrates and sulphates absorbed from the soil are utilised in the formation of those complex organic substances which chemists call proteids.

If we put the cleanly-cut stalk of a primrose-leaf (still better, that of the Chinese primrose (*P. sinensis*), so common and free-flowering in our greenhouses) into our mouth, and keep the blade of the leaf immersed in water, we can blow air through the stalk into the blade and thence into the water. It issues from the leaf through minute apertures, most numerous on the lower surface. They are readily seen under the microscope, especially on a leaf like that of the Iris, from which it is easy to peel off a film of transparent skin. They are of great importance in the life of the leaf, and are called stomata. To reverse the above experiment, the leaf-stalk should be inserted through a perforated india-rubber cork into a beaker half filled with water; the base of the stalk should be well immersed in the water. Then if through a glass tube also perforating the india-rubber cork we suck out air from the upper half of the beaker, the altered pressure induces a passage of air through the stomata of the leaf into the blade and down the stalk into the water, through which it issues as a stream of bubbles.

The recognition of these openings or stomata makes the leaf more intelligible to us. They lead into spaces within the substance of the leaf, and with a microscope it is easy to prove that they are open when the plant is in full vigour.

but that they close when drooping for lack of sufficient moisture begins, and also that they are often closed at night and open during the day. But the proof of this takes us beyond the region of simple experiment to that of microscopic observation.

By observing the rapid drooping of cut flowers, and their recovery when placed in water, or the need of constantly filling up our hyacinth-glasses, or more precisely by fixing a leafy shoot in a narrow bent tube of water, and noticing how the water diminishes when the plant is kept in a warm room, and by other more delicate experiments, we can convince ourselves that the leaves of plants give off water-vapour into the air. So much of the water which is absorbed by the roots is indeed used in building up organic substances and in growth, but by several weighings of plants it is easy to prove that much of the water simply disappears into the air. And when we consider that the surface of a leaf is often thick-skinned, and sometimes varnished with wax, and notice, for instance, how an apple without its skin dries up much sooner than one which is intact, and remember how much more numerous the little apertures or stomata are on the under than on the upper surface, we are warranted in concluding that it is by the stomata, and therefore especially by the under surface of the leaf, that the escape of water-vapour or transpiration takes place. Nor is it difficult to prove this by direct experiment. Thus we recognise another of the uses of leaves; they are the organs of transpiration, and the little apertures on their under surface, which close in drought but open when moisture is abundant, are the regulators of this.

But we have not yet completed our experiments. Let us place a number of growing seedlings in a glass retort through the cork of which two glass tubes are passed.

Connect the end of the exit tube with a glass cylinder containing clear lime-water or baryta-water, and beyond that through a perforated cork with a large vessel half filled with water. It is evident that if we allow water to flow out from the base of the large vessel, and manage the tubes rightly, there will be a passage of air from above the seedlings, through the baryta-water cylinder, into the final large vessel. As to the tube which enters the vessel with the seedlings, connect this also with a cylinder containing clear baryta-water, and beyond that with an open tube packed with caustic potash. Now set the apparatus agoing. As water flows from the base of the terminal vessel, air passes — since the whole system is continuous — through the caustic potash tube, through the first baryta-water cylinder, through the vessel with the seedlings, through the second baryta-water cylinder, into the terminal vessel. Now the air which enters is robbed of its carbonic acid gas by the caustic potash, and the continued clearness of the first baryta-water proves this. But the air which passes into the second baryta-water clouds this (with a white precipitate of insoluble carbonate of baryta), which proves that the seedlings have been giving off carbonic acid gas.

This experiment is not by any means the best that can be made in order to prove that plants, like animals, give off carbonic acid as they live, but it is one of the simplest. For conclusiveness it will be necessary to use leaves instead of seedlings, to estimate accurately the precise change of gases, to test the difference between plants growing in darkness and those in the light, and so on. But we have at least indicated how the student may convince himself that plants, like animals, breathe, — for the liberation of carbonic acid gas is associated with an absorption of oxygen and with a slow combustion of the material of the plant, as in all forms of respiration,—and furthermore, that the leaves are the organs by which the breathing is principally effected.

It is difficult to exorcise a persistent fallacy which has long plagued the student, and for which tradition and text-books are much to be blamed—that one of the great differences between plants and animals is that plants take in carbonic acid gas and give out oxygen, while animals take in oxygen and give out carbonic acid gas. This is a fallacy, all the more troublesome because both its statements are true. It is true that animals take in oxygen and give out carbonic acid gas—this is the essence of respiration. It is also true that green plants in sunlight take in carbonic acid gas and give out oxygen—this is one of their essential characteristics. But it is also true that plants, like animals, take in oxygen and give out carbonic acid gas, for they must breathe. Only it happens that in the daytime the process of respiration in green plants is externally hidden, is virtually counteracted (since much more than compensated) by the reverse nutritive process peculiar to plants. The fallacy is the contrast between a respiratory process, common to all creatures, and readily demonstrable in plants which are not green, or which are in darkness, and a nutritive process which is peculiar to the green parts of plants during the light of day.

Summary of Leaf Functions. — We are now in a position to sum up the chief functions of leaves :—

(1) Leaves are the principal organs by means of which the plants give off surplus water, and that chiefly on the under surface and through the minute apertures or stomata which regulate the transpiration.

(2) Leaves are the principal organs by means of which the plants breathe, by which the gaseous interchange which is implied in all life is effected. But during the day in

green plants the absorption of oxygen and the liberation of carbonic acid gas is counteracted by the reverse nutritive process.

(3) Leaves are the principal organs by means of which the plants absorb carbonic acid gas from the air, and by aid of the radiant energy, which passes through the screen of green colouring matter, split it up, liberating the oxygen, and using the carbon as the foundation for the upbuilding of organic products, in which water from the roots, and in some cases salts as well, are also utilised.

The student may indeed feel that these results might have been reached much more rapidly by *a priori* reasoning. As plants live they must breathe, and the leaves are obviously the organs fitted for this. As plants build up carbon-compounds, and yet get no carbon from the soil, it is evident that they must get it, as carbonic acid gas, from the air, and the leaves are obviously the organs fitted for this; and so on. But this *a priori* method is never conclusive, and though we have done little more than indicate the lines of experiment, we have shown how the functions of the leaf may be experimentally demonstrated without taking very much for granted. To do so even imperfectly is better than to follow the short cut of dogmatic assertion; and with Professor Detmer's convenient and well-illustrated manual of experimental physiology, now Englished, the student, even without a teacher, may fairly set to work, and profitably read also, as his experimental course demands, the appropriate passages in the manuals of Sachs and Vines.[1]

The Structure of the Leaf.—We are now in a position to advance to an examination—at first a very general one—of the internal structure of the leaf.

---

[1] Sachs, *Lectures on Vegetable Physiology*, Oxford, 1887. Vines, *Vegetable Physiology*, Cambridge, 1886.

The surface is often stiff and firm, and its outermost coating thick. We recognise the use of this as a protection to the delicate living parts within. When there is a waxy varnish or a covering of hairs the protection from cold and from loss of water will be all the greater. In many cases the outermost layer, especially on the upper surface, consists of units or cells with thick corky upper walls (the so-called *cuticle*), and we know how impermeable cork is to the passage of water. But in many cases the cells of this colourless layer of epidermis are very rich in water; they form a layer of little water-bags all over the leaf. We can see the use of these; they lie between the outer world and the more delicate living cells in the heart of the leaf, so that when a rapid loss of water occurs from the surface, it is not the internal parts which directly suffer, but the hardier and less intensely living epidermis.

In many cases the leaf is so well protected by its hard external sheath that there can be very little transpiration except by the regular apertures — the stomata. These are exceedingly numerous, usually several hundred on a square inch. In most leaves they are virtually restricted to the under surface, but in those of plants like the water-lilies, which float on the water, they occur where alone they can be of use — on the upper surface, and in leaves which grow upright they are equally numerous on both sides.

It is necessary to examine more carefully into the nature of these stomata. Each aperture is bounded by two special cells of the epidermis, called guard-cells. Unlike most of the cells of the epidermis, these are green, and therefore able to form starch like the tissue in the heart of the leaf. Furthermore, they are so disposed that when they are rich in water — in other words, when they are swollen, "turgescent" — the stoma or aperture between them is opened; but when the guard-cells contain for the time being less water, and are relatively shrivelled, their walls are applied to one another and the stoma is closed. The condition determining the action of these ventilators is explained then, in the first place, by reference to the state of water-tension within the guard-cells. The state of water-tension in the plant depends primarily upon the relation between the water within the plant and the external conditions of drought or humidity. Thus on dry days, when the plant is necessarily losing much water to the air, when the leaves in consequence tend to droop, the water-tension of the guard-cells is necessarily lessened, and the stomata automatically close, or partially close, thus beneficially retarding the drying up of the plant. This explanation was for a long time alone current: its insufficiency gradually became clear as observation showed that stomata in sunshine tend to open, in darkness to close; that light in fact is of more importance to their movements than is the humidity of the atmosphere. But how does the light act? It does not usually affect the opening or closing of ventilators: what can be the rationale of this strange phenomenon? This Schwendener has explained by help of their chlorophyll already mentioned; they form starch and grape-sugar (glucose) as mere epidermis cells cannot do. Hence when assimilating vigorously their glucose draws water from the neighbouring cells, they become turgescent, and so open; while, when light fails and their activity and stores diminish or disappear they close again. It seems, moreover (and thirdly), that the light, apart from its influence on the guard-cells through the formation of starch and consequently sugar, has a direct influence on the state of water-tension in the cells. We have already noticed a similar influence in the case of those plants which bend towards the light. The rationale of this has next to be sought for, and although neither so obvious or certain as in the preceding case, need not be despaired of. The varying pull of the epidermic cells upon the stomata has also to be considered, and so on.

We regard the stomata then as automatic ventilators, which have especially to do with regulating the transpiration of water-vapour from the leaf. They lead into spaces between the loosely packed cells which form the lower half of the leaf.

But where within the leaf is the important work of building up starch and proteids carried on? The answer is not difficult, for starch is a very readily recognisable substance, occurring in characteristic granules, and we know that it occurs most abundantly in the layer or layers of green cells lying immediately below the protective upper epidermis, which are so closely crowded together towards the light as to give a section the aspect of a palisade. This "palisade parenchyma" is the chief laboratory of the plant. Here it is that the radiant energy of the sun streaming through green colouring matter is used by the living matter of the plant in the splitting up of the absorbed carbonic acid, and in building up complex materials whose chemical energy is well known to us when we use them as food or as fuel.

When we think of the leaves manufacturing starch all the day long and all the summer through, the question must arise, Why do not the leaves become too full; how is it that they are not overloaded with starch? It is plain that the starch must in some way pass away from the leaves, and it is not difficult to prove that leaves which were richly filled with starch when the sun set may have very little next morning when the sun rises. When the leaves wither and die in the autumn there is again a disappearance of almost all of their starch. How does the starch disappear? in what form? by what path?

At this stage in our studies we can answer these questions

only in general terms. The starch which is made in the light cannot pass out of the leaf except into the body of the plant, nor can it pass away as such, for the solid starch grains could never get through the walls of the cells. Before it can pass from the leaf the starch has to be fermented, it has to be changed into sugar. The same is true in regard to the starchy parts of the food that we eat; it is a simple matter to masticate and swallow a potato or banana, but before the starch which these foods contain can be of the slightest use to us it must pass through the walls of the food-canal into our blood. Now the starch as such cannot pass through the walls of cells. The grains are too large. It must be rendered soluble and diffusible; in a word — digested. This process begins in the mouth, where a ferment contained in the salivary juice changes the starch into a sugar. A precisely similar digestion (by means of a ferment called diastase) takes place in the leaves, and it is in the form of sugar (glucose) that the starch passes into the stem.

But by what path? We have spoken of the epidermis or skin of the leaf above and below, of the loose arrangement of cells on the lower side, and of the always greenest palisade tissue in which the essential processes of the cell's life go on. But we have not spoken of one of the most important and characteristic parts — the system of "veins," which in most common plants forms an intricate net-work through the substance of the leaf.

These veins form the most durable part of the leaf, for in the skeleton leaves which we see rotting away in the ditches the veins persist while all else, unless perhaps the firm outermost sheath, has disappeared. There is no doubt that the "veins" form a sort of supporting skeleton for the leaf. They are the firm beams around which the more delicate substance of the leaf has been built up. But the veins are more than supporting beams; they include a system of downcast pipes by which the sugars and other materials manufactured by the leaves pass away into the stem, and another upcast system of pipes, whose necessity is equally obvious, by which the water and soluble salts absorbed by the roots and passed up the stem irrigate the leaf and supply some of the essential raw materials for the manufacture which goes on there. These two systems — bast and wood respectively — may be more fully studied when we trace them into the stem.

Palisade Cells and Chlorophyll Grains. — To the ordinary observer it seems as if the chlorophyll grains of the palisade cells had no definite position; but Stahl and others have made the very interesting discovery that a movement, at any rate a change of position of the chlorophyll grains within the living cells, may be observed when cells are brought from diffused light into intense sunshine. The leaves of the Star of Bethlehem (*Ornithogalum umbellatum* and *O. nutans*), of grape hyacinth (*Muscari racemosum*), and other common plants, notably also the lesser celandine or figwort (*Ranunculus Ficaria*), give excellent examples of this, as also do the prothallia of ferns (although here, of course, a palisade parenchyma is not specialised). In figwort, for instance, the chlorophyll grains will leave the upper and under surfaces of the palisade cell for its sides after quarter of an hour of sunshine, thus taking up a position in which they are as little as possible exposed, not only sheltered one behind the other, but with their edges to the light. When the sun goes off, they get back to their old positions, but more slowly, needing several hours. This is, of course, observed by cutting sections of leaves taken at different times.

Now we know that too much light may be injurious; and Pringsheim has made striking experiments towards the interpretation of this, showing that in a focus of intense light (from which, of course, all possibility of the destructive action of heat has been removed by stopping this off by a light transparent, yet heat-opaque alum screen) chlorophyll is at once destroyed and no assimilation can therefore go on. That different plants have different optimum light-quantities for assimilation, just as they have different optimum heat-quantities or temperatures for germination or growth, is obvious enough; but nature does not constantly supply these; how beautiful this self-regulating mechanism, by which the chlorophyll grains can utilise just their right amount of sunlight, making the most of it when it is scanty, and escaping its dangers when excessive! Nay more, may we not thus explain the peculiar shape and position of the palisade cells themselves? Is it not to give the chlorophyll granules room to assume the most favourable position that they have elongated perpendicularly to the leaf surface? In the same way, since the cells of the deeper-lying, spongy parenchyma are shaded by the layers above, and need all the light they can get for their chlorophyll grains, must not they expand horizontally? And hence we should be able to explain why it is that in shade-loving plants palisade parenchyma may even be absent, and why in shade-grown leaves the spongy parenchyma is often observed to be more abundantly developed.

The explanation is beautiful, and seems a satisfactory one; a few years ago botanists were wont to teach it without reservations. The critic, however, soon came in the person of one of our most thoughtful and physiologically-minded of vegetable histologists, Professor Haberlandt of Graz, to whom, with his master Schwendener, belongs especially the credit of attaching physiological interpretations to what were formerly too often mere microscopic curiosities. He first verifies and establishes Stahl's observations *so far*, *i.e.* in regard to some plants, insisting, for instance, on the obviousness of the phenomenon in figwort, but limits them also; these plants of Stahl's are all shade-lovers, be it noted, and no doubt specially sensitive; but in not very many plants can his observations be made. That palisade parenchyma is formed on both sides of leaves growing *vertically* is also a serious difficulty to Stahl's theory. Moreover, as to chlorophyll grains, he tells us they are found on the sides of the palisade cells whatever the intensity or direction of the sunlight; and that when they are found on the upper surface parallel to that of the leaf no change can be observed. Nor do they always present their profile to the intenser light. Hence then he gives up Stahl's explanation of the characteristic form of the palisade cells.

A new rationale, therefore, is wanted; and this Haberlandt finds suggested by a fresh observation, that chlorophyll grains are never to be found upon the *lowest* wall of the palisades (the *bottom* of the canister-shaped cells in short). Now as the current carrying off the products of assimilation (out from the cell towards the bast portion of the bundle) must pass through this wall, he argues that this is kept free for the purpose, and that this must furnish space for the chlorophyll grains, which are therefore elongated in the direction of the current. In short, the form of the assimilatory tissue (as also the position of the chlorophyll grains) is essentially adapted to facilitate the most easy (*i.e.* direct and rapid) transport of the products of assimilation, and not their position relative to the surface. The frequently radial arrangement of the green parenchyma in leaves or stems, like those of *Cyperus* of *Equisetum*, is cited to confirm this, and so on.

These two brief and necessarily scanty abstracts of Stahl and Haberlandt respectively by no means exhaust the discussion. Here, as everywhere, the aim has been to interest the reader in it, or at least to make it clear that there is one, and that scientific studies involve primarily, beside wide observation, the critical reason, not the credulous memory. Hence before leaving this subject it may be profitable to cite yet a third writer. Thus Schrenk finds cases in which chlorophyll grains do occur upon those very cross-partitions to which Haberlandt denies them, and not unnaturally urges that he cannot see how the presence of a few granules at these walls could materially obstruct the passage of the sap-current.

For him then "neither Stahl's nor Haberlandt's theories are necessary to explain the structure of the palisade cells." He reminds us of Frank's observations, that the chlorophyll grains are especially abundant in the neighbourhood of air spaces. There are of course *vertical* chinks in the palisade parenchyma, hence also the absence (or comparative scarcity) of granules at the bottom of cells, on which Haberlandt has so much insisted, becomes intelligible for quite another reason, that these generally abut upon another cell, and not upon an air space!

Discussion of this kind may seem to some unprofitable, as if there could be no certainty in physiology. Yet we should be losing one of the best lessons in biology if we failed to see the variety and complexity of its problems, and to see too how each new theorist may be doing good service by bringing some new factor or aspect of the case into view. Thus Schrenk goes on towards a compromise: "How can we imagine a plan better adapted to fulfil these two conditions (*i.e.* of access to air and to sunlight) than that on which the palisade tissue is constructed? Into a given volume of this tissue the greatest possible number of cells is packed in such a manner that each presents its upper surface to the incident rays, permitting them to pervade its whole interior, while at the same time it furnishes ample accommodation to the chlorophyll grains, on its long walls, where they have the best opportunity to come into contact with the carbonic acid in the air-passages."

This compromise the student may now himself elaborate, but also criticise afresh, so working towards familiarity with the subject.

Shapes of Leaves. — "The leaves of the herbage at our feet," Mr. Ruskin says, "take all kinds of strange shapes, as if to invite us to examine them. Star-shaped, heart-shaped, spear-shaped, arrow-shaped, fretted, fringed, cleft, furrowed, serrated, sinuated, in whorls, in tufts, in spires, in wreaths, endlessly expressive, deceptive, fantastic, never the same from foot of stalk to blossom, they seem perpetually to tempt our watchfulness and take delight in outstripping our wonder."

We do not propose to describe these different forms of leaves, nor to introduce the elaborate nomenclature which is used in order to describe them with precision; from the present standpoint it is sufficient to give a few illustrations showing how peculiar forms are adapted to special conditions, referring the student for details to Sir John Lubbock's *Flowers, Fruits, and Leaves* (Nature Series, Lond. 1888).

Large and free-growing plants which obtain unobstructed light most frequently bear simple or slightly lobed leaves, while the smaller vegetation generally produces leaves either long, simple, and narrow, as in grasses, or highly compound, with small leaflets, as in ferns and many plants of the woods and hedgerows, so as to seize as many as possible of the broken sunbeams which have not been intercepted by the loftier plants, while casting as little shadow as possible upon each other. As the same amount of leaf material has a greater surface when cut up than when forming a continuous blade, the advantage of leaf-lobing is as obvious as is the breaking up of the coast-line of a country by many fiords.

The leaves of aquatic plants, if floating, are simple and largely expanded, so as to maintain their position and obtain the maximum of light, as we see in the case of the water-lily and the pondweed. But if the leaves are submerged they are usually dissected into thread-like segments, as in the water-primrose, so as to allow the water to pass unobstructed, and thus constantly renew the supplies of carbonic acid gas.

Not unfrequently the leaves on the lower and on the upper parts of the stem are in different circumstances, and their form is also varied, as we may see, *e.g.* in *Campanula rotundifolia*, the familiar blue-bell of Scottish song (*Anglicè* hair-bell, from its thin stem, often misspelt hare-bell), in which the round leaves are only the lowest of the rosette, gradually passing to narrow "linear-lanceolate" form. A similar divergence of foliage may be seen in the water-buttercup (*Ranunculus aquatilis*), which possesses both floating leaves, which are simple, and submerged leaves, which are highly dissected. So, too, plants which grow in dry and sandy places, and obtain scanty supplies of water, either owing to drought or to the looseness of the soil, very frequently store water in their leaves, which thus become succulent, and preserve it from evaporation by a thick epidermis with unusually few stomata. The stonecrops and house-leeks of our rock-work, or the sea-shore sandworts (Arenaria, Honckenya), the sea milk-wort (Glaux maritima), and other common species of the sea-shore are familiar native illustrations; while the Agaves and Aloes, the Mesembryanthemums and Cactuses of a "succulent house" show the same habit upon the grand scale appropriate to the more extreme climates from which they come.

Let us take the case of the white water-buttercup (*Ranunculus aquatilis*) as a subject for interpretation. The facts are that the floating surface-leaves are more or less simple and rounded, and that the submerged leaves are divided into hair-like segments; and it is also known that if the plants grow in swiftly running water all the leaves are submerged and filiform, while if they grow altogether on the mud by the side of the stream the dissected type of leaf is lost and the appearance of the plant is very different. So much so, indeed, that Lamarck believed that *Ranunculus aquatilis* might thus be transformed into an allied species *R. hederacea*, but this conclusion has been denied by Godron, who has paid great attention to the variations of buttercups. It is certain, however, that the predominant type of leaf varies according to the surroundings, and that each form of leaf is advantageously adapted to its conditions. How is this to be interpreted?

Sir John Lubbock says, " Of course it is important to expose as large a surface as may be to the action of the water. We know that the gills of fish consist of a number of thin plates, which while in water float apart, but have not sufficient consistence to support even their own weight, much less any external force, and consequently collapse in air. The same thing happens with thin, finely-cut leaves. In still water they afford the greatest possible extent of surface with the least expenditure of effort in the formation of skeleton. This is, I believe, the explanation of the prevalence of this form in subaqueous leaves."

Mr. Grant Allen, on the other hand, interprets the finely-divided form of the submerged leaves to the relative scarcity of carbonic acid gas in the water.

Our view of the problem is as follows: First, we must take note of the manner in which the "veins" of the leaf are distributed in different species of *Ranunculus*, especially in those such as *R. hederacea*, which seem most nearly related to the white water buttercup. For as it is likely that the aquatic forms are derived from land forms, the established type of venation will to a certain extent limit the manner in which the leaves are cut up. The established structure of the original type must be taken into account in interpreting the derived variation.

Secondly, we should have to grow buttercups of similar origin (reared from seed or cuttings from one plant) in different conditions. One set should be placed in ordinary pond water, and another set in water with an unusually large quantity of carbonic acid gas. One set should be grown in still water, another set in the same water flowing rapidly, and so on. Only by experiments[1] more precise than those which have as yet been made, can the problem be satisfactorily solved.

Meantime we can only express our opinion — (1) that the division of the submerged leaves is determined by the established type of venation seen in related species and in the surface leaves; (2) that deficient nutrition, due to insufficient supplies of carbonic acid gas, may cause the tissue between the veins to remain undeveloped or to die away; (3) that currents of water exerting pressure upon the leaves may help to develop the filiform state; and (4) that the form of the submerged leaves may thus, in a natural and necessary way, have become well adapted to the conditions.

Leaves adapted for Special Functions. — Before we pass from the leaf we must notice some of the special functions which exceptional leaves may fulfil. Some of these we have discussed already, for the pitchers of pitcher plants, the bladders of Utricularia, the fly-trap of Dionæa

---

[1] Cf. H. de Varigny, *Experimental Evolution* (Nature Series), Lond. 1892.

are highly specialised leaves. Again, we saw that the Clematis and many other plants are leaf-climbers, and that tendrils are in many cases modified leaves or parts of leaves.

In not a few plants the leaves die away, in whole or in part, often becoming reduced into mere spines. The Darwinian explanation of course is that these spines have been produced by natural selection in consequence of preserving the plants from being eaten up by mammals. The Lamarckian explanation, on the other hand, is that spiny plants are the product of the conditions of drought in which the majority at least occur; while the writer has elsewhere [1] offered an interpretation complementary to this of thorny species as being of ebbing vitality as compared with their thornless congeners. The reader will find a vigorous criticism of this view from the Darwinian standpoint in Mr. Wallace's *Darwinism*, and (if he thereafter retains sufficient interest in these Lamarckian and neo-Lamarckian views) a briefly summarised reply in the British Association Report for 1890. The controversy would lead us beyond the limits of this little volume; suffice it here again to say that in thinking of this and many similar problems in evolution, the student should be careful to distinguish between the primary factors, which really originate the peculiarity in question, and the secondary factors, which determine whether the peculiarities shall or shall not persist. Natural Selection of course is the general name for all these secondary agencies.

Here again is a matter for direct experiment, which has indeed begun.[2] Thus Lothelier has shown with barberry and hawthorn (1) that the promotion of transpiration increases the development of thorns which were absent when

[1] VARIATION, *Ency. Brit.*, and *Life-Lore*, 1889.
[2] *Comptes Rendus*, cxii., 1891.

the plants were grown in a very damp atmosphere, and (2) that intense illumination increases spininess, while restricted illumination tends to suppress it.

In this connection may be read with advantage the plea for experiment in Dr. de Varigny's recent Edinburgh lectures (*Experimental Evolution*, Nature Series, 1892).

Very important as protective structures are the bud-scales, which are often hard and varnished, and effectively shield the tender leaves of the bud from frost and damp. We have already spoken of their importance, and have noticed that they are modified leaves or leaf-stalks, or in some cases stipules. Thus on the horse-chestnut you may find many gradations between the brown, sticky scale and the leaf-stalk with its five leaflets. Some have simply a little tip of green, in others this green tip is notched, in others it is definitely divided into five lobes.

Another special function discharged by many modified leaves is that of storing. Sometimes they are swollen with water, as in the Sedums and Aloes. Oftener they are receptacles for starch and other products which the plants manufacture. Thus the leaf-bases of the primrose which persist after the leaves die away are full of starch; and the crowded, much modified leaves which form the greater part of the bulb of an onion or a hyacinth are also storehouses, from which in spring materials for new growth are absorbed.

Some leaves are so brightly coloured that when they occur near the flower they may be mistaken for petals. We see this very well in a common greenhouse plant, the "Christmas flower" of Mexico, Poinsettia (*P. pulcherrima*); and the great white spathe which surrounds the flower of the Ethiopian "lily of the Nile" (*Richardia (Calla) africana*) is also a modified leaf.

Lastly, as every one more or less clearly knows, at least

since Goethe's day (see chap. x. p. 199), the flower itself consists of four whorls of "modified leaves"— the sepals protective, the petals attractive, the stamens producing pollen, the carpels bearing the ovules which when fertilised become seeds.

Substitutes for Leaves.— The functions of the blade of the leaf are shared to some extent by the petiole or stalk and by the green skin of the stem and branches, and often by the sepals and ovaries; in short, every part of the plant exposed to light tends to utilise it by producing chlorophyll, excepting only those parts of the flower where, in current phrase, more conspicuous colouring matters are required for the attraction of insects. Thus the green stems of Cactuses and some Euphorbias, which are practically leafless, do in a measure discharge the ordinary work of leaves. The green thorns of the gorse or whin are by no means too hardened to be of some use as leaves, and there is no doubt as to the use of the leaf-like shoots of Butcher's Broom (*Ruscus*), or of the reduced thread-like filaments (really abortive flower-stalks) of the Asparagus.

Vitality of the Leaf.— We saw that in the Indian Telegraph Plant (*Desmodium gyrans*) the lateral leaflets are in constant motion, but this is only a specially marked example of the movement which Darwin observed in all young and vigorous leaves. When we touch the sensitive plant, the petiole sinks downwards and the leaflets fold together, but this after all differs but little from the daily sleep-movements of clover, wood-sorrel, and hundreds of common plants, except in its being induced by a sudden shock. Other movements of leaves in relation to the light, as they bend towards it, or arrange themselves transversely or sideways to its rays, are of constant occurrence. We saw too that the modified leaves of insectivorous plants seemed to exude a digestive juice, but it is more important to recognise that there is, as Prof. Vines has of late conclusively confirmed, a starch-changing (diastatic) ferment in all green leaves. It is indeed in the ordinary processes of everyday life that the vitality of the leaf is most marvellous, especially in that process by which the kinetic energy of the sun's rays, entering the plant as a series of ethereal waves, passing through the screen of chlorophyll, aids the living matter to build up out of crude materials those complex organic products whose potential energy may be again transformed in heat and light or motion when we use them as fuel or food. Nor in our appreciation of the life of the leaf should we forget that it often contains enough of the plant's essential material and vigour to enable it in suitable conditions to grow into an entire plant, for every one knows how a piece of Begonia leaf, for instance, may be planted so as to produce a new plant with stem and roots.

Fall of the Leaf. — Throughout the summer the leaf lives this intense life, thriving in the sunshine, and producing a store of food-stuffs laid up in reserve in different parts of the plant. But in autumn the vitality is checked, the supplies of water which the leaves demand is no longer afforded, transpiration and the movements of the sap become very slight, and the leaves begin to die. But before they die they surrender all that remains of their life to the plant which bore them; before the breath of approaching winter all that is worth having of sugar and more complex stuffs ebbs in gentle current from the leaves to the stem. Then the leaf, useful in dying as well as in living, begins to be cut off, for while the retreat of the residues of the leaf's life is being accomplished, there has also been preparation for the leaf's fall. Across the base of the leaf-stalk, in a region which is normally firm and tough, there grows inward a partition of soft juicy cells, actively multiplying and expanding into a springy cushion, which either foists the leaf off, or makes the attachment so delicate that a gust of wind serves to snap the narrow bridge binding the living and the dead. That the scar should thus have been prepared before the operation is one of the prettiest points of the economy of woodland nature. The student may profitably collect instances of the gradual evolution of this, starting from the ordinary monocotyledons, in which no such adaptation exists.

Virtually dead the leaves now are, empty houses from which the tenanting molecules of living matter have vanished, leaving little more than the ashes on the hearth. But these ashes — how glorious! for in yellow and orange, in red and purple, the leaves shine forth, glowing in the low beams of the autumn sun.

Sometimes it is the green chlorophyll which breaks up, and leaves little heaps of yellow grains which gladden our eyes in golden leaves. Sometimes, on the other hand, amid the flux of molecules inwards from the leaf, there appears a special decomposition product — a pigment of death — anthocyan, which along with the acids so often present stains the leaf with red, or without the acids gives us bluish-purple, or along with the yellow grains above mentioned shines out in bright orange.

Then the leaves, flushed in death, fall gently from the trees, or writhing and rustling in the wind, as if loath to be separated, are finally wrenched off and scattered. It is the curfew of the year, and the poets listen mournfully to "the ground-whirl of the perished leaves of hope, the wind of Death's imperishable wing."

But as the species lives on while individuals die, so the tree is hardly impoverished when the leaves fall from its many branches. Over the broken parts the partition membrane completes its healing salve and protective scar, while the fallen leaves, weathered, faded, and torn, are mouldered by fungi and bacteria, covered up by the earth-worms, and gradually form the soft mould in which are born the seedlings of another year.

CHAPTER X

SUGGESTIONS FOR FURTHER STUDY

Root and Stem — Flower, Fruit, and Seed — The Web of Life once more — Systematic Botany — Morphology of Organs and Tissues — Evolution.

Root and Stem. — The general idea of the function and structure of the leaf which we have now obtained, obviously prepares us to ask questions as to the stem and root. How does the leaf get its water of transpiration, its salts of assimilation? And as these have obviously to be absorbed before they can be carried up to the leaf, it may be literally as well as metaphorically most profitable to begin "at the root of the matter." Let us watch then the growth of rootlets in germinating barley, in a hyacinth and a potato, each in a hyacinth glass and the like. Let us carefully wash away the soil from a well-grown pot-plant, to get an idea of the enormous development of the root-system, while the attachment of the fine root-hairs to the particles of soil may be readily studied under the microscope from a gently washed seedling of grass. Thus questions will accumulate: How do these root-hairs absorb, and what? What elements are essential? Or again, in a different order of ideas, How do roots grow? The former is a matter for physical and chemical experiment, the latter for observation, helped of course by the microscope; and thus the student can work on, his scientific progress being in proportion to the degree in which he finds he can ask reasonable ordinary child-like questions; a degree which he must not be discouraged to find probably at first inverse to that at which he could "get up" a large amount of ready-prepared information upon the subject. In the same way let him ask questions of the stem, and devise, even if he cannot always execute, experiments. How is the stem constructed? will be best understood if he does not begin with the book, but by scraping and slicing at a few twigs of laburnum, ash, lime, and oak, till he has seen all that naked eye and lens can see, and so on. Then the anatomical detail of the text-books will become of interest, and therefore of true service; it helps to clear up how the stem works as well as how it grows; and thus the simple outline but complex detailed discussion of the "circulation of the sap," of the "thickening of the stem," and the like, becomes gradually familiar and interesting. From simple outlines, like those of *Stem* and *Root* in "Chambers," the student may in fact pass direct to Detmer's experimental handbook, and to the convenient survey of the question of sap-circulation in Marshall Ward's *Timber and Timber Trees* (Nature Series, 1889), and to that of stem-structure in his little book on *The Oak* (Modern Science Series, 1892); thence returning to the larger text-books.

Flower, Fruit, and Seed. — Leaving now the problems of vegetative life for those of reproduction, of self-maintaining for species maintaining, a new field of study, the most fascinating of the science, opens before us. Here again, beginning with the actual floral procession of the year in fields and garden, we gather and inquire; our books, always kept in subordination, mere accessory helps to the study of the phenomena themselves. If the student be by this time willing to take the writer for examiner, he will be asked, as always, not to answer questions — with second-hand information — at the end of his day's work; but to ask questions — about such actual flowers and fruits and seeds as he can see — at the very beginning; this done, it is the books and the teacher whom *he* has to examine, the limits of *their* knowledge which it is his business to work up to and to define. He must look how flowers are arranged before "reading up *Inflorescence*"; and take them to pieces before reading of sepals and petals, of stamens and ovules; he must puzzle about what pollen and ovules are for, he must watch the bees and butterflies among the flowers, and find out which flowers no insects go to, before reading of insect- and wind-fertilisation; then the books of Grant Allen and Sir John Lubbock may be read one summer as pleasant introductions to the larger volume of Hermann Müller (the standard work of reference upon the subject) for the next. Finally its bibliography, supplemented by that of MacLeod,[1] is exhaustive. Kerner's *Flowers and their Unbidden Guests*, and his *Pflanzenleben*, now being translated, will also be of special interest.

This widening knowledge of flower-function will of course involve an increasing minuteness of observation in detail, and the Darwinian interpretation of the utility of even the smallest of these — the shape and relative position of parts, the colour, the markings, the perfume — will give them interest. Thus arises a knowledge of flower form not only far more interesting and more genuine, but more permanent and more intimate and thorough than that of the conventional "anatomy before physiology" method, against which this little volume is a continuous protest. For it is only when we have first seized the essential parts of the flower (stamens and carpels), and seen how they are adapted

[1] *Botanisches Jaarboek*, vol. ii.

to cross or self-fertilisation, and thereafter the petals and sepals, as at best accessories to this main function, direct or indirect, mechanical or attractive (if not largely subordinate to mere external and protective purposes), that our morphological interpretations can become either safe or clear.

Coming in the same way to the study of the fruit, let the student at first severely leave alone the competing classifications, the arid and excessive nomenclature of the text-books, and ransack the fields and garden, the fruit-shop too, if it be summer-time, the latter at least if it be winter. To crack an almond and find out what corresponds to its shell and kernel in cherry, plum, and peach, is no hard lesson; precisely to compare any of these fruits with a pea-pod may at first puzzle the beginner, but the pleasure of the discovery will outweigh its pains; or similarly to ascertain exactly wherein they agree with and differ from apples and pears, and to make out for oneself the interest in this whole connection of the fruit of *Cydonia japonica*, so commonly grown on walls for its beautiful scarlet apple-blossom. What is a raspberry? how does it resemble and differ from the cherries and plums when ripe, from a strawberry when young? What *is* a strawberry? Is not its flower practically the same as that of an apple? Think out, then, how this wide difference (yet deep resemblance) of fruit must arise. Again, what is it that we eat in the orange? Dissect it carefully, and look at it in water. Return for more light on the question to the unlikely pea-pod; if this does not readily reveal its open secret, go to the bean! The subject abounds with fascinating puzzles of this sort, some easy, some difficult; in fact, as the rose family well show, the fruit often tends to be more Protean in variety than the flower. These asked and answered, or at least honestly puzzled over, any new set of specimens, say a handful of beechmast, hazel-nuts, and acorns, becomes as welcome and interesting as it could be to a child. Sir John Lubbock and Mr. Grant Allen again offer a pleasant guidance to the Darwinian interpretation of the fruit, while the simplification of nomenclature and the common sense of classification may be conveniently entered by help of Chambers's "FRUIT." Similarly with the study of Seed we must start with observation, say with our almond again, and work out a new chapter of our scientific education.

The Web of Life again. — Our chapter of the web of life dealt with the vegetative system almost alone, yet was complex enough; here the introduction of the reproductive system makes the drama a far more complex and fascinating one. Each plant, in fact, like man himself, has many relations to the world around, and the botanist thus becomes a biographer of each; yet though materials abound, the full life-history even of the commonest plants has still to be written; and the student, as Prof. Balfour has well pointed out, may do good service to science by following this from seed to seed again, and year by year.

Here then is an incentive to the study of the complete flora; since every plant is not merely a new specimen to be preserved or analysed, a new beauty to be admired, but a new life, with an individuality and a history of its own. From landscape we come back to foreground, from the idea of *vegetation* to that of *flora*.

Systematic Botany: its Methods and Results.— To examine our individual specimen and recognise it with certainty is a matter needing no small precision in detail; we have to draw with accuracy, and to describe with no less precision, the criterion of a good description being that a drawing can be prepared from it by a draughtsman who has never seen the plant. One is constantly asked by some friend returning from a walk or greenhouse visit the name of some plant whose beauty has excited a momentary enthusiasm, but cross-examination leaves in nine cases out of ten its beauty wholly indistinct: not a word of intelligible (*i.e.* intelligent) description can be given. Here is a real disclosure of deteriorated observing power, of utter vagueness of memory and language, on which the conventional educationist would do well to ponder, and which is by no means limited to things botanical.

This matter of systematic botany is in fact one which the most strictly linguistic of educationists would do well to consider. Limits of space prevent any adequate presentment of its advantages; but the proposition may be formally advanced, with definite offer of detailed evidence to any teacher who cares to inquire further into the matter, that here is assuredly a subject from which the accurate use of language may be rapidly and surely learned (probably more rapidly and surely than from any other study); clearness and order, precision of details yet subordination of these in respective rank being carried out here — thanks to Linnæus — as in no other science. Here, however, a mere suggestion must suffice; so let the reader try to write a description for himself of primrose and snowdrop, violet and hawthorn, daisy and dandelion, so that a correspondent, say in tropical India, should be able to tell what they were like; then compare these with the descriptions in the appendix of Lindley's *School Botany* (a treatise well worth hunting for through old book-shops), and see whether botany has not something to teach him in the use of language, and what is the real need and justification of scientific nomenclature.

Systematic Botany. — We have not only to describe our plants, but to name and classify and group them; and here again begins the vastest chapter — say rather literature — of the science. How we are to name, and why we must name in the universal language; what are the difficulties of this problem, and what its history; what the advantages of the binomial nomenclature, defined and organised by Linnæus; and what we are to understand by the much disputed terms of species and genus—here are some of the initial questions to be asked. Again, how shall we arrange our genera into larger groups, of order, class, sub-kingdom, and the like? How did botanists classify before Linnæus? What was his essential work, and what was the character of his *Artificial System?* How was his work continued and developed by his school, and how far was it altered and improved upon in the *Natural System* of De Jussieu? What of the subsequent development of this?

Nor can we answer these questions without asking more. The most concrete way of doing this is, returning to the landscape and foreground, the vegetation and flora, of our former problem to endeavour to make from these an ordered whole—a botanic garden; or if this may not be, at least a *hortus siccus*, a herbarium, which, because of its very dryness, may readily become far the completer garden of the two. Still the garden has even more advantages than the at first sight obvious ones, and as space forbids even outlining these, it must suffice here to press upon the student the desirability of discovering these by experience. A botanic garden need not be on the scale of that of Kew or Edinburgh; a small college may have its acre or two, a school its rood or two, an infant school its pole or two, even the dismallest of town schools its window-boxes now, as by and by its little conservatory. For help as to practical details, the student or garden-loving teacher may safely apply to any botanist of his acquaintance, or failing such acquaintance, to the writer, who has annual experience of this kind.

Some account of the vegetable kingdom can be obtained more easily than any other botanical information, although even here again, as so often, better in foreign text-books than in English ones. Warming's *Systematische Botanik* will serve the student as the best guide to Baillon's *Histoire des Plantes* and Engler and Prantl's more full and recent *Pflanzenfamilien*, while a more modest acquaintance can be obtained from any of the ordinary manuals, large or small. The article, "Vegetable Kingdom," of Chambers's *Encyclopædia* and the *Britannica* may also be consulted; with their minor articles on the particular natural orders and on special plants; while the historical evolution of this field of science is outlined in Chambers at BIOLOGY, BOTANY, and BOTANIC GARDEN.

Morphology of Organs (Comparative Anatomy). — With our widening survey of plants increases our knowledge of bionomics, our grasp of individual and general physiology, but also our anatomical knowledge and skill. We thus acquire a wide acquaintance with the *forms* of leaf, of stem, and root, as well as with their life; why should we not generalise this knowledge also, and consider each of these organs apart from its function; so developing a highly abstract science of "pure morphology" — a crystallography, as it were, of the organic world? A leaf in the physiological sense we saw to be the organ of transpiration and assimilation; but a stem may do the same, even an unearthed potato. Shall we define it by its usual form, its bilateral symmetry, its two surfaces? But to these characters there are many exceptions; and, moreover, stems may flatten out into what are, in general aspect as well as function, excellent leaves. Seeking a yet more general character, we say, morphologically speaking, leaves are *appendages* of an axis — the stem, *i.e.* arise upon it, and never from each other. Now arises a new set of physiological difficulties, well seen in the prickly pear. Here the great flattened joints, so like huge succulent leaves in appearance and function, are branches, *i.e.* secondary axes; the true leaves are here the prickles. *True*, however, is here an unsatisfactory and only half-true term; in this contrast between form and function we have at the earlier planes of evolution what in our own plane we recognise so constantly as the difficulty between law and equity, letter and spirit. *De jure* it is the prickles which are the leaves, since historically and formally they represent them; no matter though *de facto* the stems have long ago taken up their whole functions. In the same way the Merovingians are kings *de jure*, long after their mayors are kings *de facto*. Here, in fact, we have a curious result, carrying with it a fresh result upon the theories of education; for the student may easily think out for himself the way in which we may either start from the one side or the other. That the "type system of teaching," with its precedence of anatomy over physiology, is no mere survival of the authority of Cuvier, but is in a piece with the antique academic programmes generally, he will now more clearly see; as further, that the "life-history" (as distinguished from "form-description," or even "form-history") system of teaching here advocated, with its precedence of physiology before anatomy, while in the first place an attempt at utilising the method of Darwin in biological teaching, is congruent with those wider changes in education now happily germinating everywhere, and of which this University Extension movement, with its published volumes, its enlarging summer meetings, may claim to be one of the largest seedfields.

Returning, however, to pure morphology, although no outline can here be given, some notice must be taken of that generalised conception which has been prepared for in the preceding paragraph, since it is the most characteristic, or at least the best-known, result of the science.

We have seen that the young flowering-plant — the seedling — consists of an upward-growing axis or stem and a downward-growing axis or root, and that the young stem bears on its sides one or two seed-leaves or cotyledons. Here we have the simplest form of higher plant — an axis with appendages.

And when we study the various appendages which are borne by the upward-growing axis or stem, we see that they are all fundamentally the same. The seed-leaves are not unfrequently of the same general type as the foliage-leaves; the latter are connected by gradations with the scales which are wrapped round the buds, and the bracts which lie at the bases of the flowers. The transition from bracts to calyx may be conveniently studied in the mallow, that from sepals to petals in the cactus, that from petals to stamens in the water-lily or in almost any garden rose (which, indeed, appears to have suggested the whole theory) and that from leaves to carpels in many monstrous flowers, especially the double cherry. Almost every one has seen some flower or other in which all the parts had reverted to the state of green leaves.

For further corroboration of this idea that all the appendages of the axis are fundamentally the same in structure, or are, in a word, "homologous," we must watch the development of these parts. In so doing we find the theory adequately confirmed; leaves, bracts, sepals, petals, stamens, and carpels all develop as precisely similar processes of cellular tissue from the sides of the axis.

This conception of the plant as an axis bearing variously modified but homologous appendages, floated before the eyes of Wolff and Linnæus, was more clearly grasped by the poet Goethe, was systematised by De Candolle, and has since been corroborated and amplified by the progress of morphology. See MORPHOLOGY (*Encyclopædia Britannica*).

Morphology of Tissues. — But axis and appendages

alike consist of first embryonic and then developed *tissues*, the same which in the leaf we have already learned to know as epidermic, fundamental, and fibro-vascular. The study of these in all their forms and modifications, from the physiological and the morphological point of view alternately, the continued analysis of tissues into *cells*, and the fuller study of this ultimate unit-mass, and of the *protoplasm* of which it is composed, is the new subscience of histology so important to physiology and morphology alike. Were new chapters (say rather volumes) available, we should work out generalisations of no less interest and value than any preceding ones; we should study the growth and development of the plant by the multiplication and differentiation of its primitive embryonic cells; and we should trace these back to the fertilised parent cell or plant-egg, and though the simple morphology of protoplasm would yield us little, its physiology would carry us far. See CELL of "Chambers," with Bower's *Practical Botany* as convenient laboratory guide to the larger manuals of Van Tieghem and De Bary, etc.

It is not, however, with this last product of analysis that our studies would close; we need a returning physiological synthesis. That is to say, we should trace our initial egg-cell onwards into organism again; this, however, no longer viewed from without as a specimen or form for analysis, but as a *working thought-model*, and this in actual growth, change, and evolution. The reader's knowledge of the leaf, for instance, has to be built up into such a mental image. The up-stream of transpiration has not only to be *seen* by itself, exhaling its rising fountain into unseen spray, the stomata adjusting their openings meanwhile, but this must be combined with a picture of all that we know of the process of assimilation and its resultant downward stream; so with the whole plant, so with its changes throughout the year, so with the living world. In this process of scientific imagination let the student by all means *examine* himself; he will thus not only find how little he knows more surely than on more customary methods, but feel keener interest in filling up the blanks in his knowledge; nay, even make far more rapid and more permanent progress, since we remember what we want to know far better than what we get without asking. This habit learned, the student may, with increasing advantage, direct his own further studies.

Evolution. — The student who has thus from the outset been at the evolutionary standpoint will have little difficulty in continuing his reading. Summaries which may be of service in reading the *Origin of Species* and other essential literature of the subject, together with some outline of the state of contemporary discussion, will be found in the writer's articles DARWINIAN THEORY and EVOLUTION of Chambers's *Encyclopædia*, and VARIATION AND SELECTION of the *Encyclopædia Britannica*. Mr. Wallace's *Darwinism* and Dr. de Varigny's *Experimental Evolution*, both already mentioned, notably of course also Mr. Romanes' *Darwin and After Darwin*, may next be read; and from these it is easy to gather references to the remaining (often more or less anti-Darwinian) literature. But in this, more than in any previous field of study, the student will need to keep his own faculties, observant, critical, and reasoning, fully alive.

THE END.

.

www.ingramcontent.com/pod-product-compliance
Lightning Source LLC
Chambersburg PA
CBHW020912230426
43666CB00008B/1423